*sixty*something

*sixty*something

A positive handbook for the third age of life

DR JOAN GOMEZ

Thorsons
An Imprint of HarperCollins*Publishers*

Thorsons
An Imprint of HarperCollins*Publishers*
77–85 Fulham Palace Road,
Hammersmith, London W6 8JB

First published by Thorsons 1993
1 3 5 7 9 10 8 6 4 2

© Joan Gomez 1993

Joan Gomez asserts the moral right to
be identified as the author of this work

A catalogue record for this book
is available from the British Library

ISBN 0 7225 2758 6

Typeset by Harper Phototypesetters Limited,
Northampton, England
Printed in Great Britain by
Hartnolls Ltd., Bodmin, Cornwall

For those who have achieved it and those who live with them, work with them and love them.

Contents

Chapter 1

Taking stock

'The best is yet to be,
The last of life, for which the first was made.'
Robert Browning

So – you've arrived. At 18, 30 or even 45, 60 seemed past it: definitely old. But now you realize that you are still the same person, with hopes, fears and loves – as always. Age is not just the length of time since you were born, your legal, chronological age. It is much more complicated. How old do you think you are? Judging by:

1. Your appearance,
2. How well your body functions,
3. Your lifestyle, what you do,
4. Your thoughts, attitudes and interests,
5. What makes you laugh,

– and finally, deep down inside, what age do you really feel yourself to be? That's what counts. Don't be misled by the attitude of those around you, who don't understand the facts. They may include your children, your colleagues, even your family doctor. My two eldest daughters, normally highly critical, took me out on my birthday. They were horribly kind.

'You've done so well with your life,' they said. I could see that they thought it was rocking-chair time for me.

I prefer to think about people like Red Adaire. At 73 he

was the only man with enough experience, expertise – and guts – to cope with the difficult and dangerous task of controlling the fire on the Piper Alpha oil rig: the practice run for Kuwait. Karl Wallenda walked the high wire, a hundred feet up, in his 70s; while Claudio Arrau continued to delight us in his 80s at the concert piano. Among the distinguished women who will never see 60 again are Professor Dame Margaret Turner-Warwick, President of the Royal College of Physicians in London, Dr Anne McLaren, Director of the Medical Research Council, and the novelists Penelope Fitzgerald and P. D. James. And none of these people is a health freak – so take heart.

You are not at the beginning of an inexorable decline, to be endured, but at the dawn of the next stage in your development, to be enjoyed. It is rather like when you left school. Natural enough to feel a quiver of apprehension, uncertain of what lies ahead – but count up all the difficulties you've come through so far. This is a challenge, with the chance of building something worthwhile. You are entering the training period for the next 20 or 30 years, a time of greater freedom of mind and spirit than you have ever had before. Aim to get the maximum out of your opportunities.

Factual reminder

Your brain and body have such gigantic reserves that even if you lose a chunk through wear, there will still be more than enough to make up. For example, a woman's ovaries contain enough potential eggs for 400,000 babies. You can donate a whole kidney and not miss it. And there's a 24-hour built-in repair service to deal with any damage. Time isn't the top enemy. It is neglect and lack of use that lead to rusting of your mental and physical assets. Practice is guaranteed to increase your mental range farther than ever before, and put into reverse much of any muscular fall-off.

Use it well and your equipment won't let you down.

To begin with, make a tally of your advantages. The key words are freedom and experience. With normal luck you will have fewer dull domestic responsibilities: less cleaning up, shopping, chauffeuring and providing meals for others. You are out of the rat race and the fight for promotion; you don't have to search for a mate or a home. You don't have to worry about getting pregnant, you or your wife; and your children are as independent as they'll ever be.

The other big plus is experience. Whether you are in the later stages of a full-time working career, or one of that increasingly rare breed, a home-maker, you will have learned a lot about people. The golden gifts of tolerance, understanding and tact may now be yours: spiced with realism. You will no longer be disappointed when other people turn out to have human flaws. You will also have acquired more knowledge, more skills, and a wider vocabulary. When you run into problems you haven't met before, the chances are, with your experience, you've dealt with something similar.

A third big advantage is demographic. Your age group is a growth area, increasingly recognized. The Editor of *Woman's Weekly*, a top-selling women's magazine was recently celebrating the fact that their main readership was among the over-45s. Advertisers, travel agents and even employers are waking up to the facts. One major university centre has instituted a policy of hiring 'mature' secretarial, administrative and catering staff because of their reliability.

The marvellous technological advances of the twentieth century, including those in medicine, are tailor-made for you: from the automatic gearbox to the answerphone. They cut down on boring physical exertion – and time. With a simpler, less effortful lifestyle you are able to choose what you do with a larger proportion of your time, energy and funds. Evidence: the majority of modern-day explorers are the over-60s. They include the ubiquitous American widows. You meet them up the Himalayas, down the Nile, North in Reykjavik, South in Santiago . . .

Run through some of the things you would like, right now. Health and happiness go without saying, and harmony with others is a useful backdrop. If your marriage or any other relationship needs a springclean – attend to it now. Then turn your mind to everything you've ever wanted to do, or learn or see, but could never fit in. Include some of them in the life-plan you'll be making.

Before getting down to the planning proper, check out your personal equipment: body and mind. Since you cannot trade either of them in – even if you'd want to – view them as you would a 1930 Rolls Royce: valuable, serviceable, interesting and good-looking. It – or you – deserves reasonable maintenance, repairs if necessary, correct fuelling for the vintage, and competent driving. Expect some signs of use, but also smoother running: in your case because of mellowing and experience. Newer models may get from 0 to 60 quicker, but you will have the more comfortable journey.

Your huge advantage is that, unlike a car, your body and brain will adapt continuously, in both their structure and their working, to meet your changing requirements. But you have to signal what you want.

PERSONAL ASSESSMENT

To be on top form for the great adventure ahead you need to have an idea of your current situation – physical and psychological.

Physical tally

- In general can you manage to do about as much as most people?
- Can you climb two flights of stairs, not hurrying, without getting short of breath?
- Is your weight within 15% of the ideal? See the chart on pages 231–2.
- Can you cope without taking any regular medication?
- Can you enjoy what you consider a good meal?
- Do you take exercise several times a week? Walking briskly counts, but most household and gardening chores do not.
- Have you smoked any tobacco in the last five years?
- Do you drink more than 14 units of alcohol in a week, or 21 units if you are a man? A unit is half a pint of lager or beer, a single measure of spirits, a glass of wine or a small glass of sherry.
- Do you have plenty of chips, cheese, fries, dips and spreads, nuts, pâté, red meat, chocolate and pastries?
- Have you any particular weak spot: back, feet, digestion, chest, bowels or water?

Count 2 for every YES to the first six questions, and take off 1 for every YES in the last four. A score of 6 or more means a pass, but special care needs to be taken if it is lower.

Psychological tally

This has three sections.

1. *Intellectual*
- Have you any interests outside your work or your routine activities?

- Are you ever enthusiastic about something?
- Can you concentrate on tasks or on reading that interests you?

A YES to any of these gives you a flying start. List some of the subjects you know about: those associated with your main occupation or general subjects. For example: car-driving; cooking; sport; music; nature; antiques; politics, etc. You are probably more accomplished than you thought.

2. *Social*
Make three short lists:

- Clubs, societies, groups, religious bodies, to which you belong.
- Friends: those you are actively involved with, those you see occasionally, and those you really ought to do something about.
- Neighbours whom you know, know by sight, and other possible contacts.

This is your basis to build on.

3. *Emotional*
List your family members, near and remote.

- Whom do you love among your relatives and others?
- Who loves you?
- Who needs you?
- Who at least accepts you?
- Any pets?

This is the area which gives you a sense of worth.

Preliminary general plan

Jot down how you would like to see yourself in five years' time:

1. *Main occupations:* work or work-related, and pure leisure activities.
2. *Material concerns:* clothes, home, other possessions, travel, theatre and everything that costs money.
3. *Personal relationships:* with your partner, relatives, friends, neighbours – and other people.
4. *Special extras:* preferably not repeats, nor trips down memory lane, but experiences you feel you've missed out on. Perhaps you have a yen for dinner at the Waldorf-Astoria or the Ritz, to go into Local Government or write a thriller, to play the guitar – or see Niagara?

With a general idea of your long-term objectives and an overview of your present situation, you are ready to fill in some practical details for working towards what you want.

Your body

You have to convey to your muscles, joints, heart and lungs that, far from pensioning them off, you are expecting good service from them for many years to come. The way to get the message over is by exercise. You may not have been able to fit it in systematically before, but now you are more in charge of your own timetable you must make a slot for it. Be realistic. You are not going to reach Bruno, Woosnam or Navratilova standard, however hard you train. Choose your exercise with these objects in mind:

- Pleasure.
- Maintaining your muscle power and mobility.
- Warding off osteoporosis, circulatory problems and constipation.
- Keeping a trim shape.
- The social spin-off.

CONSIDER: angling; badminton; boating; bowls; croquet; cycling; dancing; fencing; golf; keep-fit; orienteering; pitch & putt; pony-trekking; snooker; swimming; table tennis; tennis; *walking*, including rambling, bird-watching.

AVOID: jogging, squash and marathons (because they are more strain than gain); aerobics classes; team games; charts and targets (since they often lower morale).

Exercise you should certainly avoid, because of its propensity to cause real damage, is sudden and sustained, and with an emotional content: pushing a car up a hill, lugging a heavy case across an airport concourse to catch a plane, or moving heavy furniture.

If you are keen on sport and sports people, but some circumstance prevents your taking part, why not grab the social side anyway? Coaching and refereeing children and amateurs, or taking on secretarial or catering responsibilities for a club makes you part of the scene.

Your brain

While this is not the stage to take on fresh, highly demanding physical activities, your brain will thrive on stimulus: new interests, new subjects to study, new people to talk with and exchange ideas. You cannot overload your intellect or wear it out, but it appreciates change. This is why school timetables are divided into lessons on different subjects, rather than, say, a day or a week on English, then one on mathematics. Recent research has shown that new problems to tackle stimulate the brain cells – at any age – to develop more communication links.

Unless you allow dry rot to set in you can go on mastering new concepts well into your mid-80s. You must inform your mind, even more urgently than your muscles, that you require it in full working order, and that you will be sending it the nourishment of new ideas frequently, from now on. If you have been in the same post for years, or, for that matter, running a home and family, you will have become so expert that, to a large extent, you can operate on autopilot. You don't have to refer to a textbook or the government regulations or a cookery book to do the job. This makes for smooth functioning but doesn't spark off curiosity or enthusiasm.

Work and similar occupations at 60-plus are considered in Chapter 8. Meanwhile, this is also your intellectual development period for Stage 3 of your life (Stage 4 comes later, from, say, 87). It involves jettisoning some old habits of thinking and some restrictions, and instead, expanding your skills and interests. Barring accidents, your mind is fully capable of coping.

Start by researching into what is available locally: for instance literary, scientific or historical societies, bridge or chess clubs, writing, art or musical circles, one-off lectures, classes or adult education institutes. Are there any that appeal? If you don't want to feel committed to attending regularly, consider a correspondence course in leisure, general interest or potentially saleable subjects – with or without a diploma at the end. Whatever you decide to try, back it up with a reading programme and radio.

Some of what is on offer

Arts: Architecture, antiques, cartoons, drawing, painting, photography, poetry, creative writing, calligraphy.
Crafts: Carving, cookery, crochet, dressmaking, embroidery, marquetry, massage, picture framing, pottery, restoring furniture or china, tapestry, woodwork.
History: General, of art, local, ancestry.
Languages
Literature: (including that of other cultures).
Music: Playing, singing; music appreciation.
Nature: Birds, plants, gardens, herbs, the countryside.
Psychology: Assertiveness, general, child, self-development, stress management.
Oddments: Computing, public speaking, stamp collecting, stars, theatre, acting.

Boredom is the enemy: it means tension, frustration, restless dissatisfaction – and the temptation to eat, drink or smoke when you shouldn't. Welcome the challenge of different ideas and different people. You will gain by an advance in knowledge, a greater understanding and a growth in character.

The interest you take up will become a kind of companion – as painting was to Winston Churchill: 'Painting is a friend who makes no undue demands, excites no exhausting pursuits, keeps faithful pace even with feeble steps, and holds her canvas as a screen between us and the envious eye of time.'

Your feeling self

'No man is an island . . .', and no more are you. Just as much as the reasoning part of your mind needs mental activity to sustain it, so there is another part that starves without interaction with other people. At this stage in your life there is a danger of your becoming deprived on this front. Retiring from work cuts you off from contact with a whole group, while at home a more gradual reduction in contacts occurs.

Contemporaries may use their own 60-plus freedom to bury themselves in the country – miles away. Older relatives may move on into rest homes and beyond. Your children have flown the coop and no longer fill the house with their friends. Finally, your finances may be a limiting factor on social activities. In your master plan, allowance must be made for this as well as natural wastage.

Even among those of us who profess to prefer our own company there is an underlying need to feel worthwhile, to belong somewhere. For this reason, aim gradually to build up a reserve of people you feel comfortable with. One obvious way is to spend part of your time working outside your home, voluntarily or paid: see Chapter 8. Courses you follow and interests you develop will provide contacts with whom you have something in common. You may have paid a subscription for years to a club or society without getting much value for your money: now is the time to put that right. Your favoured political party, Church or synagogue, a charity that requires other help than just donations: any of these may enrich your acquaintanceship. Sharing a leisure-pleasure is an excellent beginning.

If you are naturally reserved, remember that other interesting people may be diffident, too. At your first meeting, reassure other people that you are well-disposed, and would be happy to know them better. Determine – on principle – not to be racist, sexist, ageist or any other discriminating-ist. You are adult enough to be open-minded and tolerant – especially now you are not trying to cultivate a long-term career, nor compete for a lifelong mate.

Weave a safety-net of friends and acquaintances, then you will have no need to put a strain on the precious relationships you have with those you love for the sake of simple companionship. We all like to feel loved and wanted by, for instance, our children, but beware of generosity with strings attached.

> Anne and Jim wanted to see more of their grandchildren. They offered to pay all the expenses of a shared holiday with their son and his young family. They chose a hotel they knew to be very comfortable, but geared more to the middle-aged than toddlers. While they were away Anne took the opportunity of advising her daughter-in-law on child care, from her store of 1950s experience. Jim was open-handed with ice-creams and sweets 'for the kids', regardless of their mother's frowns. The holiday didn't work out, but not because of lack of love on either side.

Although the younger generation do not always, or for long, enjoy our company, there is a wealth of appreciation and affection to be tapped from those within ten years either side of our own age. Our opinions, company and advice are of value to them – and vice versa. Make a slot for them in your schedule.

Personality and character development

Forget any notion of your personality becoming set rock-hard and immoveable. The next 20 years will involve substantial changes – in you. You have the choice whether these are positive or negative. We all know people who become increasingly selfish, mean or judgemental and others who withdraw into often hypochondriacal isolation. The negative groups abide by old-fashioned, rigid rules and, since the rest of the world does not do the same, they are constantly disappointed and disgruntled.

How much more satisfying to develop the ability to understand other people's viewpoint. Not merely what you would want in their situation, but how an insecure, inexperienced manager – or mother – of 23 might see things. Your life-experience allows you to enter into the feelings of a 10-year-old, a brand-new parent, or a 40-year-old being turned down for the job he or she had set his or her heart on. Your empathy is genuine. You will also have learned the art of coping with a world that isn't black and white – and certainly not grey. Situations, people and problems come in a complex multicolour mix.

Is a surgeon who works selflessly to improve the lives of his patients, but is selfish and uncaring at home, good and kind or callous? Deliberately to kill another human being is wicked. Or are there circumstances which would make it the correct action? It is only at your level of maturity that you could simultaneously congratulate and commiserate with a man who had won a million. Your mind can encompass, and you can live with, all the contradictory factors.

A bonus will be your better understanding, at last, of your own parents, among others. Everything that has ever happened to you involving people will have taught you a little more about them – and about yourself. Added to these automatic developments in character, you may determine to practise, for instance, showing more patience, or to nurture your feeling for nature, history or beauty.

Role count

If other people appear complex, consider how many roles *you* have learned to play – and are still performing. Here are some of them which may apply to you:

- man or woman
- partner
- parent
- gardener
- cook
- carpenter
- knitter
- expert in – your work subjects
          – your extra interests
- teacher
- philosopher
- peacemaker
- and most important, a model for the generations coming up.

Responsibilities

Your main responsibility now, as it was when you were 20, is to yourself: your own health and happiness. Without these you will be in no position to help your partner, an ageing parent, your children or any others that look to you. Whether you are the helpmeet of a man who resents retirement or of a woman who feels she has lost her importance in the home, the first essential is to raise your partner's self-confidence. This calls for tact and self-control. The more successful you are, the less will your effort and care be recognized.

Confidence doesn't come from exhortation, but from achievement. The trick is to induce the other person into some activity, however simple. Never say: 'Why don't you do X?' or 'If I were you, I would do Y.' To get them going you have to ask for help in doing whatever it is. Another ploy is to ask for your partner's opinion – on any subject. And when you have a discussion you, of course, will usually be right, but don't win every argument when you are trying to raise someone's confidence.

With a definitely aged relative you have to steer a course between being patronizingly kind and impatiently critical, but there is satisfaction in using the personality and skill which come from being 60-plus.

> Alfred, 92, likes to talk about Gallipoli in the well-worn phrases the family know by heart. He needs a listener because this was the most terrible experience of his life, and he still needs to come to terms with it.

We who are 30 years younger can understand and allow for his need, and equally we are able to answer an acute cry for emotional support from a 25-year-old neighbour whose cat has gone missing. We are at a wonderful age, with minds and hearts enriched by experience so that we have the beginnings of wisdom; and there are years ahead in which to live our lives to the full.

Chapter 2

What to expect: physically

'White was his beard as is the daisy,
Of his complexion he was sanguine . . .
To live in delight was ever his wont.'

Geoffrey Chaucer

Your body isn't stupid. It has a mind of its own – the autonomic nervous system – with centres in the brain and spinal cord. It works in conjunction with your body, responding to its every need 24-hours-a-day, all at a subconscious level. You don't have to think or arrange for digestive juices to be poured over food arriving in your stomach. You don't have to calculate how much to raise your blood pressure to supply your brain adequately when you get up from a sitting position.

Your body's control system does not deal merely with the minute-to-minute adjustments required. It adapts to the different demands put upon it at different phases in your life. For instance, at your present age, if you are a woman, it does not need to pour out sex hormones in a never-ending rhythm of periods on the off-chance that you might want to become pregnant. If you are a man it's likely that you've moved beyond the stage when all you had to offer at work was energy without experience. You still want to be fit, but not to live by your muscles.

Your body has been changing and adapting to your

needs all your life, and this will continue. You can expect
gradual, subtle modifications to provide efficiently and
economically for your 60-plus lifestyle. To get the best
results, the smart move is to chime in with any changes,
not battle against them. Take golf. An accurate swing and
a touch of cunning will give you a more satisfying game
than belting the ball two hundred yards into the rough.
Since we can chart the probable changes in advance, we
can also plan how to co-operate with nature and sidestep
any inconvenience.

Bones and teeth

This isn't the time for heavy manual labour, so you don't
need such a substantial chassis. Reduction in the size and
weight of your bones began when you were nudging 40.
If you are a woman you no longer have to store extra
calcium in your bones for building an unborn baby or
manufacturing breast milk. The good sense of having
lighter bones means they cost less effort to carry around.

Risks: Your bones may lose too much of their substance,
including calcium, and become brittle. If you are a
woman and had an early menopause or hysterectomy,
you are particularly vulnerable. For men the major risk
factors are the generous use of tobacco and alcohol,
impairing the absorption of calcium and other nutrients.
On the plus side, if you are black you are likely to have
top-grade, robust bones through your genes.

Action: Ideally you should start this before you are 60, and
just continue. Bones need protein and calcium: hard
cheese and sardines provide plenty of both. Green
vegetables also contain calcium as well as vitamin C,
another requirement for healthy bones. The sunshine

vitamin, vitamin D, is also necessary. Your body can make and store its own supply of this, especially on your summer vacation.

A word of warning: unless you are prescribed it by your doctor, don't try to top up your vitamin D with supplements from the pharmacist. Unlike vitamin C, your body cannot get rid of an excess of vitamin D from a concentrated preparation. It has particular dangers for our age group, since it can cause hardening and calcification of the arteries, and kidney stones. You can come to no harm taking your vitamin D the natural way – from salmon, sardines, herrings, eggs, cheese, butter and margarine.

The other essential is exercise, particularly walking. Your bones, like other body tissues are constantly being renewed, and exercise is the stimulus that keeps them strong. A shortage of the female sex hormone, oestrogen, weakens the bones.

This is through loss of collagen, which normally gives the bones their toughness. Various forms of hormone replacement therapy (HRT) are available. It needs to be continued indefinitely, but is not suitable for everyone, and is a matter to discuss with your doctor. Lastly, especially men, watch your tobacco and, to a lesser extent, alcohol use: they interfere with absorption.

Teeth

Teeth are, of course, harder than ordinary bone, and are designed to last 200 years! Nowadays dental surgeons are so knowledgeable and skilled that more and more people are keeping their natural teeth for life. Over time the enamel gets thicker, which gives it a darker hue. This is perfectly healthy, and harmonizes with the darkening of the skin in the 40s and 50s.

Risks: You might think that tooth decay, and drilling and filling, are things of the past. No such luck. The period from 60 to 65, like the years 15 to 20, is a vulnerable period for teeth. Problems with the gums are also common, since they tend to shrink away from the teeth slightly. Similarly, if you have had dentures for several years the lower set in particular may have become loose or ill-fitting, because of shrinkage of the jawbone.

Action: It is important for your comfort, your smile and your digestion that you have efficient teeth. If they are natural, continue – or start again – having dental checks once or twice a year. With dentures, every two or three years may be enough. If you are having trouble, there are new techniques for anchoring a wayward lower set. The saliva becomes thicker with the passage of time, and you may find your mouth uncomfortably dry. This is one of several good health reasons to drink plenty of fruit juice and water.

Diet has a place in everything: apples (peeled if you have dentures) provide first-class exercise for teeth and jaws. If you have heavily-filled teeth, partial or complete dentures, don't tempt fate by eating toffees, nuts, tough meat or anything rock-hard. Choose your dishes sensibly at a restaurant so that you don't have either to swallow unchewed, indigestible chunks of food or to risk damage to your teeth.

Joints

It's only to be expected that some wear and tear arises in the moving parts of your body. Anyone over 35, in fact 60% of men and 44% of women, are likely to have X-ray evidence of this in the lower back, even without symptoms. Your knees are likely to complain if they are carrying more weight than they had bargained for, while both hips and knees may have suffered extra strain if you've been a sports fiend, or had an accident, maybe years ago which jarred the joint surfaces.

Risks: These include arthralgia, meaning aching in the joints, or arthritis, frank inflammation. They are a nuisance, but in no way dangerous.

Action: Use all your joints, but don't go in for marathons – either spring-cleaning or the sporting type. Or, if you must, go into training first. Joint stiffness, not arthritis, can be gently exercised away. Most of us over 40 feel more supple after we have been up and around awhile in the morning. Jogging may be good for the circulation, but it jars the ankle joints – so walk or swim instead. The big breakthrough is the help, for women, of HRT. It is the collagen that deteriorates and makes the joints stiff and painful. HRT has now been shown gradually to restore the collagen in skin, bones and joints. You can start HRT at any age after the change and go on to any age, so long as you have cleared with your doctor that you are not one of the few for whom it is unsuitable. Work on male HRT is under way. Otherwise, take mild exercise and keep your weight within reasonable bounds. Fish liver oil or plant oils in your diet do not lubricate your joints.

Muscles

Muscle power peaks at 20, then stays virtually the same for the next 20 years – unless you take up a totally sedentary existence. From 40 through to 70 there is a slow fall-off in sustained power and muscle size, especially in men, but your grip remains as strong as ever indefinitely. After about 70, the big muscles tire more easily, but the finer movements of painting, sewing, playing the piano are as good as always. Think of Michelangelo painting the ceiling of the Sistine Chapel at 80, or Yehudi Menuhin today, still drawing magic from his violin.

Risks: There is only one: disuse atrophy. Disuse is more dangerous than age: a marriage that limits your sports activities, and an absorbing white collar job combine to make you neglect your muscles. Astronauts have the same problem. Weightless in a confined capsule, they have to guard against muscular deterioration by an exercise programme. It is good sense to do the same.

Action: Physical conditioning will make you feel generally fit, and will specifically preserve your muscles so that they are as serviceable at 74 as at 50. The muscles respond to regular reminders that you need and value them – not to two weeks' activity holiday after 50 weeks slugging around, nor to a spate of heavy digging when the spring sunshine tempts you into the garden after a winter's hibernation. Miss out marathons, jogging and squash, and don't be fooled into pedalling an exercise bike. Unlike road-work it only involves a few muscles, and gives you a sore seat into the bargain. Housework and gardening don't count many pluses, and are liable to cause backstrain.

Consider golf, tennis, cycling, badminton, swimming – and walking in every form.

Heart and circulation

Barring accident or illness (dealt with in Chapter 4) you can rely on your heart to pump indefatigably for as long as you need, getting supplies of oxygen and nourishment to the farthermost outposts of your body. Rhythmic contraction and relaxation is in the very nature of the heart muscle cells. The only change over time is that your heart as a whole becomes slightly stiffer, so that it responds less rapidly to emotional or other messages to speed up or slow down.

Peak output from the heart pump, in relation to body size, occurs at age ten, and goes down by 25% by age 60. The rate of pumping slows dramatically during childhood, settling at around age 20. From then onwards it slackens pace almost imperceptibly, levelling off in the 70s. My mother's pulse, at 94 is rock-steady at a standard count of 80 beats a minute. Anywhere from 50 to 100 is normal, according to the American Heart Association.

Blood pressure, by contrast, while it hardly changes from 20 to 40, increases gradually from then on. This is because the arteries carrying the blood away from the heart become less stretchy over time. A plus from this reduction in elasticity and the similar changes in the heart itself is that, unlike adolescent soldiers on parade, you are not likely to faint from an unstable blood pressure going down. On the other hand, you may notice that it takes a moment or two for your circulation to adjust when you get up from a low chair. This requires your heart rate to increase. The watchword is to give your heart warning of what you want – by rising without a rush. The warm-up before an exercise session comes into the same category. In the longer term it makes good sense to build up an exercise routine in advance, if you are planning, for instance a holiday in the mountains.

Your coronary arteries, which supply the heart muscle itself, are hardly affected at all by age alone. What may damage them are the traps of the affluent society: smoking, a sedentary lifestyle and a fatty diet in an overweight person.

Risks: Being 60 doesn't involve any particular circulatory snags, and your heart will co-operate with all reasonable demands. You haven't been able to undertake great athletic feats since you were about 30, but there is plenty left to do.

Action: The consideration your heart and circulation require comprises moderation with fatty foods, alcohol and salt; no smoking if at all possible; regular exercise; and ways of finding mental relaxation.

Breathing system

The breathing apparatus partners the heart and arteries in supplying the tissues with vital oxygen. It also provides the power for speech, singing – and laughter. Because of its two roles it has two control systems: one which runs automatically throughout the 24 hours and another that you switch on at will. The first maintains your breathing, awake or asleep, increasing or reducing the rate according to current demand: you can override this and hold your breath, or use it to produce sounds.

The capacity for conversational speech continues indefinitely, but if you are a singer or a public speaker you may find it tiring to sound off at full volume, so enjoy the convenience of the microphone age. Your lungs, like other parts, lose some of their elasticity over the years, and your rib muscles are slightly less strong. Your diaphragm, the sheet of muscle dividing chest from abdomen, and the most important for breathing, remains in excellent condition. Your metabolism is fractionally less demanding at this stage, and you can expect your lungs to bring in all the oxygen you want, without effort.

Risks: The only snags are smoking and certain illnesses.

Action: To keep your breathing apparatus healthy you

must, of course, avoid the self-supply of pollution by tobacco. Regularly spend some time out of the atmosphere of central heating, which dries the delicate membranes lining your breathing passages. It is helpful to get into the habit of standing up straight. It is good for your appearance and gives your lungs maximum freedom to expand.

Digestive system

This system is likely to be as good now as ever it was, and a source of pleasure indefinitely. You may be making slightly less stomach acid, but that does not prevent your deriving all the nutritional value from your food. Some substances are absorbed a little more slowly at 60-plus. For instance, aspirin and paracetamol may take a few minutes longer to have their effect: a matter of patience. Sugar, calcium, vitamin C and thiamin (one of the B group of vitamins) are also less easily absorbed, so you need to keep up the supplies: with cheese, fruit, muesli, and wholemeal bread.

Risks: Indigestion, susceptibility to ulcers and other illnesses.

Action: As for any adult, neither alcohol, cigarette-smoking nor strong tea or coffee is kind to your stomach. Filter coffee is more irritating than instant. With time and money your tastes may have become more sophisticated. Meals can be too lavish, too large, and washed down not with fruit juice but with too much wine. Bear in mind that this is the same apparatus that you were using when you were ten. Would your present diet have suited it then?

The bowels

This is another part which doesn't deteriorate just because of half-a-century's service. The muscles of the colon have not become smaller and weaker, in which they fare better than the ordinary muscles that are under your control. Nevertheless, it is only fair to co-operate with your waste system. The somewhat less active life you lead now, compared with when you leaped before you looked, can affect your bowels in two ways. Since you are less physically active, you no longer eat the huge amounts you required as a teenager: so there is less waste matter for your colon to get a grip on. Secondly, your outer abdominal muscles, that used to hold your tummy flat, tend to stretch over time, and give your colon less support.

Risks: Constipation, bloating.

Action: To keep your colon happy make sure of plenty of fibre in your food. This is also an insurance against colon cancer. Useful foods are porridge, muesli, All-bran, natural bran, wholemeal, leafy vegetables and such fruits as oranges, plums, prunes, figs and bananas. Regularity in your mealtimes is also beneficial, especially breakfast. A bowlful of hot porridge makes an excellent stimulus for bowel action. Concentrated nourishment, with little residue, such as chocolate, cheese, cakes, pastries and potato crisps, is no help at all. The other ploy is exercise that involves your abdominal muscles: swimming, walking and specific exercises like sit-ups, leg-ups or 'cycling' on your back. African or oriental heredity confers a more efficient, quicker acting colon than that of white westerners, quite apart from diet and lifestyle.

Harsh purgatives that galvanize the bowel are rarely wise and often have a rebound effect. If you need to help your colon on a temporary basis, retrain it with a preparation of ispaghula husk like *Fybogel*, or a similar provider of soft extra bulk.

Bloating means that your abdomen swells up during the day, however little you eat. Then maddeningly, it goes flat overnight. Often too energetic an effort to keep up your fibre intake is partly responsible. It is important for bloaters to avoid leguminous vegetables (peas and all kinds of beans) cabbage and natural bran.

Water system

The key organ, the kidney, has such a huge reserve capacity that it will function effectively into your 90s, unless there are specific problems. High blood pressure, smoking and bladder infections (cystitis) may cause some impairment.

Risks: From a mechanical point of view, from about 60 onwards two forms of nuisance may slowly develop. In men the prostate gland normally enlarges a little. It may press against the exit to the bladder, so that the outflow of urine is slow and incomplete. Alcohol makes it worse. See Chapter 4 for the effective medical answer.

Women have no prostate to worry about, but particularly in those who have had children problems of water control may sneak up. You may find you can't wait, even when your bladder isn't full, or that you leak a little when you laugh or cough. This is so common as to be normal, but is obviously distressing. A family doctor or gynaecologist can direct you to a bladder exercise nurse to learn how to strengthen the internal muscles. A mild, unrealized bladder infection is a common cause of problems (see Chapter 4). Care of the normal system is outlined below.

Action: As with other plumbing systems this one benefits from plenty of water flowing through. This can come from fruit juice, mineral and tap water, tea and coffee. An excess of caffeine-containing drinks stimulates your kidneys, like a diuretic: overstimulation is tiring. Alcohol is also a diuretic and a direct irritant to the bladder. While it is a treat for you, it isn't for your water system – so compromise.

Skin, hair and nails

Your skin and hair are always on show, so they matter. While your skin tends to become thicker, and for that reason darker in the years from 20 to 45, at 60-plus there is a reverse trend. The skin, like other parts, is involved in the body's economy drive: the reduction of non-essentials. Your skin now is becoming thinner and more delicate, more liable to injury. Some of the fat that fills it out is jettisoned. More important, the collagen fibres which give it elasticity began to break into shorter lengths, and are less efficient: but only in the exposed parts. That is why lines appear on your face but not on your body. The more you are exposed to ultra-violet light – by sunbed, Mediterranean or Californian-power sun, the greater the effect. Plastics, too, become brittle left outside.

The cells containing melanin, the brown skin pigment, may bunch together and form freckles on your hands, but in general they become fewer at this stage. The lubricating glands, producing oily sebum for your skin are also less in number: bonus: you never see a 60-year-old with acne, and seldom with a shiny nose. Another plus point is a reduction in one type of sweat gland, the apocrine. These are the type that the deodorants aim to control. The other sweat glands produce an odourless secretion.

One result of having fewer sweat and lubricating glands is dry skin. You may find it peeling in tiny flakes, or, particularly over your shins, it looks shiny and dry. This is nothing to worry about, but such skin is asking for care. Men in general have a tougher skin, more durable than women's, and best of all is the Caribbean quality: young-looking and serviceable indefinitely. Asian skins are next best. If you are lucky enough to have either of these skin types, instead of having to switch to pastel colours as your skin becomes paler and more delicate, you will look good in any colour you like, including vivid reds and yellows, until you are 90 and beyond.

Risks: Dry skin, which can often be itchy; wrinkles; little, scaly sunspots – on bald heads and other exposed places.

Action: Avoid intense, direct sunlight and artificial ultraviolet, and use a first-class sunscreen whenever you go out in the summer. To prevent your skin from ageing it is worthwhile to use a sunscreen on the exposed parts of your skin winter and summer, even in England. Use bath oils but not detergent bubble baths, and be generous to your face, neck, forearms and shins with petroleum jelly lotion (*Vaseline*) applied morning and evening. Expensive creams and lotions, containing vitamins and hormones in some cases, are likely to be less beneficial, while those which are perfumed can be harmful. For women the collagen-preserving effect of HRT by tablets or implant is worthwhile, however.

Too much alcohol, smoking and to a lesser extent coffee and tea, coarsen the skin and speed up the wear and tear process. Vitamins C (fresh fruit and salads), E (vegetable oils, soya, eggs and peanuts), and beta-carotene (carrots, tomatoes, bananas) are all beneficial to the skin. It is preferable to get these from food rather than tablets, since concentrated preparations can have side-effects (see pages 215–19).

One area of your skin that deserves special consideration is a part that you feel but seldom see: your feet. Patches of hard skin and corns can be their revenge for

WHAT TO EXPECT: PHYSICALLY   37

badly-designed and ill-fitting shoes, worn for elegance. Most feet appreciate the kindness of shoes a half-size larger, with low heels – like those worn by the young these days. Cold feet, the forerunner of chilblains are due to another form of cruelty to feet. Thin shoes and seven-denier nylons are fine for an outdoor party, but not for going shopping.

Hair: As with your skin, your hair becomes more delicate and fine, and may lose some of its colouring matter. This latter is obviously something you can combat chemically if you wish, but beware of sensitivity to a dye. Have a limited trial to start with, in a small inconspicuous area. Very few of us retain as thick a head of hair now as 20 years ago, especially if we are red-heads, but frank hair loss is practically confined to men. It is linked to heredity and a plentiful supply of male sex hormone. There is now an expensive lotion containing minoxidil which can improve male pattern baldness in most cases: but you need to continue using it for life, and there may be long-term side-effects which have not yet emerged.

  Also, as with your skin, your hair is likely to be less well-lubricated than before: it will certainly not become lank and greasy. Frequent washing with mild shampoo, and the occasional use of an anti-dandruff type, whether you have dandruff or not, plus a creamy conditioner will keep your hair healthy. If you have lovely white hair don't let anyone, not even you, discolour it by smoking.

Nails: If your nails have become a little rougher and more brittle, the chances are that you are short of iron rather than calcium. Rev up your intake of any of these: liver, red meat, spinach without added water, watercress, soya, chocolate, sardines, dried fruit. Vitamin C helps you to absorb iron, but too much wholewheat, tea, eggs, oatmeal and cornflakes tend to prevent this.

The senses

The sharpness of any of the five senses may be modified over time, but not to the same degree, nor necessarily noticeably.

Seeing: The lens of your eye is an improvement on a camera lens: not only does it concentrate whatever you are looking at onto the retina at the back of your eye, but it is flexible enough to change its shape. Like other parts of the body, it may become stiffer, in some people from age 40, in others never detectably. The effect will be a difficulty in focusing on books or papers which are close. Reading glasses are the easy answer. The other change is in the colour of the lens, so that what you see through becomes slightly yellower over the years. This is so gradual you will not be aware, but it is interesting to compare great artists' early paintings with their later ones. Rembrandt's self-portrait in old age is yellowish compared with the first such.

Cataract, a step further than the normal changes in the lens structure, is dealt with in Chapter 4, page 79. Another troublesome normal change, noticeable especially if you spend much time in a polluted atmosphere is recurrent soreness, and sometimes watering of the eyes. This indicates that you are producing quite enough tears to keep the front of the eyes well-washed. There is a simple answer in 'artificial tears' (see Chapter 4, page 79).

Hearing: As for singers, your difficulty, if any, is likely to be with the high notes. Even in our 30s we usually lose our ability to hear a bat's squeak, or a 'silent' dog whistle. Ordinary conversation generally presents no problems, but with some voices or at a lecture or the theatre you may find yourself having to strain to make out the beginnings and the ends of certain words. Or you may start missing the telephone occasionally. This is the signal to have a hearing test.

If there is a fall-off get a hearing aid now. The modern types are brilliantly effective and so small as to be barely visible. The benefit of getting an aid while you are still young is that your brain will more easily learn which sounds to edit out. At first, with an aid you will be aware of such sounds as a ticking clock, which you had previously been unable to detect, and would prefer to keep out of consciousness.

The other disadvantage of delaying the use of a hearing aid, if you need one, is that you will find yourself increasingly irritated by other people seeming to mumble. The loudness of the lower notes, in the middle of the words will be just as always, but you'll miss out on the identifying consonants. This is how the slightly hard of hearing come to ask others to speak up, and then complain that they are shouting (see Chapter 4, page 80).

Taste, smell and skin sensations: you will have no trouble with these senses, but if you have a relative in their late 80s or older, they may have blunted sensations. Older people may miss a smell of gas, or burning, and may be slow to notice their skin temperature going down in winter. The good point is that their sense of pain from a cut or bruise is less sharp.

Metabolism

Your metabolism comprises the chemical processes going on in your body continuously, particularly the use of fuel and oxygen to provide you with warmth and power. The metabolic rate is the speed with which you use your fuel. There is a drastic reduction throughout the growing-up period, and a very gradual slowing by about five per cent during the whole of time from 25 to 65, in the *basal rate*. This means when you are doing nothing active.

There is likely to be more of a contrast in the total metabolic rate over these years, since you will probably be doing less physical work, or doing it in a more leisurely way. Walking at 4 mph burns twice as much energy as ambling at 2 mph. Since your rate of burning fuel (food) has gone down, your body will require less, or less concentrated forms of nourishment. Where you might have scoffed a burger in a bun at 25, a banana might now fulfil your body's needs. At this stage you are free to indulge in fruits and vegetables, and instruct your appetite accordingly.

A farmer in Vermont in 1902 consumed 3600 kcals daily without getting fat. Today a male executive aged 30 is likely to take in 2700 kcals, and 2050 kcals at 65, while women run at a lower level: 2000 and 1800 kcals respectively. These figures are those found best for survival by the Life Insurance companies for men on average 70 ins tall, weighing 154 lbs (70 kg), and women 64 ins tall, and 120 lbs (55 kg).

A Reasonable Diet: A section on diets for different purposes is found on pages 222–30.

Individual taste is your major guide, but you can help this by trying different dishes from among those now thought to be 'good' for us and our modern lifestyle. Thomas Parr, whose tomb is in Westminster Abbey, is said to have lived 152 years on a diet of coarse bread, cheese and whey. A recent diet, constructed by nutritionists in Edinburgh, covers all the normal nutritional needs at 60-plus.

Breakfast
Fruit or juice
Cereal with semi-skimmed milk
Toast or roll with margarine or butter, marmalade or honey
A drink (tea, coffee, chocolate) with semi-skimmed milk

Mid-morning

A drink with a piece of fruit if desired

Lunch

2–3 oz (60–90 mg) cheese, fish, meat, chicken or an egg
Vegetables or salad – with dressing
Roll and butter/margarine or potato in jacket
Fruit
Beverage

Mid-afternoon

A drink with biscuit or fruit

Supper

4 oz (120 mg) meat, fish, poultry
Vegetables including potatoes, or salad, dressing if desired
Bread or roll and margarine/butter *or* biscuit and cheese
Dessert or fruit
Glass of wine sometimes
Water
Coffee

Bedtime

Milky drink, biscuit

Chapter 3

What to expect: mind and brain

'Call him not old whose visionary brain
Holds o'er the past its undivided reign:
For him in vain the envious seasons roll
Who bears eternal Summer in his soul.'
                                Oliver Wendell Holmes

In the areas of thinking, feeling, understanding and knowledge you have everything to celebrate. On the physical side there may be changes that limit your range, but on the intellectual and emotional fronts you will continue to grow and develop, through all the years ahead.

Of course, you can help yourself to achieve your fullest potential, but, unlike the situation with your muscles, you don't need to aim merely at maintaining what you've got. Now is the time – and the opportunity – to explore your own untapped depths and discover buried talents and richer understanding. With an estimated ten billion neurones (active nerve cells) in your brain, you have more than enough to allow for all possible natural wastage, plus reserves to cover most accidents or disease.

Louis Pasteur did much of his most important work after having suffered several strokes. Mother Teresa, 80-plus, with heart and circulatory problems, retains immense emotional strength and mental stamina. And don't we all enjoy watching – on the TV or the stage – those wonderful elderly actors and actresses, compared with whom you are a young spring chicken?

Intellectual aspects

It used to be thought that becoming older, particularly past 60, meant an inevitable decline in mental ability. Government departments in the United Kingdom and most European countries enforce an arbitrary retirement age, not applicable to politicians themselves, of course. Since many of the most prestigious, responsible and lucrative posts in industry are held down by those in their 60s and 70s, it is understandable that green-eyed younger others propagate the myth that all their seniors must be past it. The United States and Sweden have long since outlawed blatant ageism in employment, as part of the Equal Opportunities legislation.

Since the mid-80s research has provided clear evidence that age alone does not cause mental decay. But it does involve change: towards different stratagems of thinking and solving problems. These only become possible with substantial experience of life. Piaget, the greatly revered developmental psychologist, believed that there was no advance in the way the mind works after about age 15. Believe that and you can't have lived!

The standard IQ (Intelligence Quotient) tests were designed for assessing children and adolescents, and are geared to their capacity to learn the basic know-how to fit them for adult life. This is what youngsters need. Adults like us require much more subtle and wide-ranging powers. Even the Primary Mental Abilities Test, which divides intelligence into so-called fluid and crystallized components, fails to test for creativity, responsibility, administrative and executive abilities, ethical judgement

– and common sense. This latter is the practical application of urgent problem-solving skills.

Examples

> Your son or grandson, 17, has just passed his driving test. He wants to borrow your Mercedes to impress his girlfriend. He has studied hard this year, and is a sensible youngster.

> The dog has eaten three-quarters of the joint you are about to serve to a dinner party of eight. Your guests are already downing their aperitifs.

> You have arrived to open a new technical institute, not your particular area of expertise as a businessman, and you find that your secretary has put the year's financial report in your folder instead of your speech.

Do you really think a 15-year-old could cope as well as a 60-year-old in these circumstances? And what about the old desert island scenario: who would you choose as your sole companion: an electronics whizz-kid of 20 or an old buffer of 60-odd with years of Army experience behind him? Even for a 1000-mile trip across Europe by motorway your chances of arriving in one piece would be much higher with a driver in his 60s than with a youth – however sharp his reaction times.

Stages in intellectual development

Until the second half of the twentieth century the expectation of life, especially healthy life, was cut short by infections and heart diseases in particular. It may have been partly because of this that until recently psychologists thought there were only four stages in human mental development. A fifth stage, representing intellectual maturity, is now recognized. The first three stages are all concerned with getting what is needed for survival during childhood. Stage four, the so-called formal operational stage develops after puberty and involves ideas and imaginative possibilities: what would happen IF?

These four stages lead up to the well-worn methods for solving problems: collecting together the relevant information, then focusing on it systematically to produce the simplest solution. This is called convergent thinking, the type assessed by IQ tests. What you are now able to do is divergent thinking, related to de Bono's lateral thinking: less mature adults cannot grasp the method. It involves accepting and incorporating various contradictions. An obvious example is your nearest and dearest: this person can give you more delight than anyone else and cause you more grief. Other people are good and bad according to circumstances, who else is around, and the subject in question.

Real-life, human problems are often to do, not so much with grey areas, but a rainbow spectrum of multi-colours. Several answers are simultaneously partly right. You've only to try running a children's party to work that one out. When you were psychologically immature you would not have been able to put yourself in someone else's place, especially in a disagreement. You could only see what you would feel, if it was yourself in the other person's situation. Have you never been woken at 5 a.m. by a beaming child, bringing you the 'treat' of a slopping cup of lukewarm tea in bed?

Only now are you truly grown-up, because you've experienced what it feels like to be five, or 15 or 45. You've lived through hopes and disappointments, failure and success, love and rejection – or fear of it. Only now can you imagine being small and weak, or ambitious but insecure, or the other sex. Hand-in-hand with this flexibility of understanding is your mature perspective. You can see much more clearly what really matters.

You are less inclined to be distracted or distressed by what the people next door will think, or by a plan that doesn't work out, or losing money – so long as the people you love are safe. The arts of compromise and try-again are part and parcel of the mature approach. It is because of this gift, not available to the immature, that an exasperated young executive, in difficulties with administration, said: 'Hell, I'll just have to make way for an older guy.'

It must mean something that the peak age for leadership in business, politics, diplomacy, and academia lies between 65 and 69. The highest earners and financially most powerful are almost all between 55 and 80.

Learning and memory

It is traditional to expect anyone over 50 to be forgetful, and for the victims themselves to get into a near panic if they have a lapse of memory. Is this to do with age, the beginning of a downhill slide? Absolute rubbish: think back. Can you remember a child, perhaps yours, who left his book or his blazer 'somewhere', or forgot to give you a message from his teacher? I guarantee he didn't say: 'My God, I'm losing my marbles. Of course, at ten years old I should expect it.'

When you forget things – like other people – it is probably because you weren't paying attention, something else distracted you, or it wasn't particularly interesting. But if you've become sensitized, every normal slip of memory will be emphasized in your mind. By all means make lists if you wish, to make assurance doubly sure, but ten to one you won't need them except psychologically. Both short and long-term memory work as well as ever, but particularly in the over-80s the co-ordination between the two may be less precise. The mass of material in long-term storage gets out of proportion with the short-term store, which only covers a few days at any one time.

Some medicines, especially the benzodiazepine 'tranqs' and 'sleepers', interfere temporarily with memory. The most frequent difficulty is with names. This is because there's no logic in them: how many Bakers do you know who actually make bread? To say nothing of names like Carruthers or Bush.

Learning

Simply don't believe it if someone tells you it's difficult to learn anything new when you are over 60, otherwise how do all those older actors manage? My mother, whose only education was a village school in the early years of this century, was widowed at 78. Feeling disinclined to marry again, the usual career for women of her generation, she decided to learn the subject and open an antique shop. During the first year she made a few mistakes, but by the middle of the second she was making enough to rent proper premises. She became an expert in Victorian watercolours. She retired at 90, but only after a serious operation.

The Open University has countless examples of students of so-called retirement age obtaining degrees.

Numerous psychological studies have shown that – so long as they are not hustled or hassled – older people, into their mid-80s learn perfectly well, often mastering a new subject more rapidly than younger people. The motto is 'Take your time' if you want to learn effectively. It is when your brain is relaxed and unhurried that it will function at its best. Don't try too hard and you may well get there ahead of the crowd. Some subjects are a natural for our age group: statistics, history, literary criticism, metaphysics, psychology and writing fiction. These all seem to require a long experience of solving problems. Like sport, mathematics in general is for the under-40s, but there are always exceptions.

When you are learning a practical skill, you will fare better with hands on, trying it, rather than listening to instructions first, which suits other age groups.

Problem-solving

As you might guess from your learning style, at 60-plus you will have developed a particularly good practical sense. Experience has taught you this, as well as a selection of short-cuts. You are much better now at getting directly to the heart of a problem, than you were, say, ten years ago. Theoretical problems with no relevance to people won't stimulate to the same extent, however.

Having puzzles and problems to work out acts like a fertilizer to your brain. Brain cells that lie around unused don't die, but neither do they go on forming new connections with each other. Feed them regularly with reasoning tasks and their communication system is stimulated – like that of a successful business.

Creativity

The mix of imaginative and productive skills that underlies music, art, writing (prose or poetry), scientific research, entrepreneurial business and philosophy is a vast area that IQ tests don't touch. Original and unconventional thought is the province of the very young and the fully mature: the former because they haven't learned the accepted rules yet, and us because we've grown past them.

It is sometimes assumed – wrongly – that young adults hold a monopoly of creativity. For example, while most scientific research is carried out by the comparatively young, and often published in their name, the original concepts frequently come from their professors. In medicine 50% of the advances have been made by those over 45.

In the arts those 20 or more years older than we are have continued to do wonders of creative work. Picasso was painting controversially in his 80s, while Titian did some of his best work at 90. Goethe was 80-plus when he finished writing Faust, and Verdi the same age when he composed Aida. Stravinsky's creative career spanned his early to his very late adulthood, while Stokowski signed a new recording contract in his 90s. The philosopher Bertrand Russell was full of fiery ideas at 60, 70 and 80 onwards. Galileo made the original observation of the oscillation of the moon in his 70s, Thomas Hardy was writing poetry in his 80s, while Tennyson, in his mid-70s published his Ballads and his play Becket. Fontane, like Mary Wesley now, did not start writing his best novels until he was 70, and Jessica Tandy won an Oscar for a film role when she was over 80. The list is endless.

You have plenty of time, and the capacity intellectually to achieve of your best. But this is a matter of choice. You may value most the basic aspects of living: the people in your life, your home and Nature in your garden and out. But you don't need to feel limited by any crazy notions of mental decline.

Before going on to take a look at the enthralling changes and developments you can expect in the spiritual and emotional parts of your mind, take a final look at thinking and reasoning. What are the possible snags, and how to deal with them?

Risks

Top risk is mental rust from disuse, often based on lack of motivation and loss of confidence, in turn due to ageist attitudes in society. When I left a voluntary job I'd much enjoyed, because 'it is policy to retire our workers at 60', I was given a party. Everyone said 'Goodbye' as though I were going on a journey: but I wasn't going anywhere. They gave me a lovely book with pictures of rural England, in case I forgot how to read. There were no woolly bedsocks, though.

When I got home I rushed to a mirror to see if I'd aged terribly since morning. I seemed about the same. I plucked out a grey hair, anyway. We must resist the attitude of other people who don't understand, and discard their quaint values. They've got it wrong.

Apart from definite illnesses, there are some physical risks to the efficient working of the brain: alcohol, tobacco and overweight. Medical problems which can interfere include, commonly, diabetes and high blood pressure, both eminently treatable.

What you must do for a healthy brain

For starters, cut down on drink, smoking and eating if any of these has crept up unbeknownst; and ensure that exercise and fresh air supply your brain with blood and oxygen. For lack of motivation, there is only one cure: achievement.

Confidence-raising exercise: You don't have to do anything difficult. Set yourself one task each day that uses your brain, and write it down. At the end of the day, tick off the completed task: You can then go to bed knowing that you have done what you specifically set out to do, whatever else has happened in the day. This way you build up the sense of achievement, the confidence that you will succeed in anything you put your mind to.

Don't choose activities that depend on the weather, or someone else, or that are too difficult or complicated. You'll think of better tasks for yourself, but here are some starters:

- A trip to the library: a treasure hunt.
- Reading a chapter, an article or a poem.
- Listening critically to any piece of music.
- Write a letter, friendly or business.
- Examine a building or some natural feature, and describe it in a hundred words.
- Find out what classes or talks or exhibitions are available locally.
- Re-organize a drawer, cupboard or room.
- Fix up to see a friend for an exchange of ideas.
- Listen to an informative radio programme or watch a documentary.
- Send off for a correspondence course.
- Make a reading, listening or viewing plan.
- Visit a museum or gallery.
- List your good points and advantages.

Of course you'll do all manner of useful things in the day, but the nub of the exercise is to achieve, for certain, the one item you decided on.

Like training your voice or your muscles, the name of the game is 'practice'. Exercise your mind regularly, at first gently, then with increasing purpose until you have found a subject that interests you. All of history, all of humanity are there for you. Especially seek out something fresh to you, something you haven't done before, somewhere you haven't been, different people or those whose paths diverged from yours long ago. These provide the refreshment the thinking part of your brain needs. Boredom is the enemy; a new interest is a new friend.

Emotional and spiritual aspects

Your intelligence remains at your service, ready to adjust to new problems, new challenges. But your feeling and spiritual mind is really coming into its own during this period ahead. You have had first-hand experience of the dreams of childhood, the idealism of adolescence, the hopeful plans of early adulthood, and maybe the joys and the torments of parenthood. It is no accident that judges are appointed at a mature age, when they have acquired the capacity for emotional detachment from their work problems, but not from their feelings for their families.

They – and you – can keep a cool head, assess other people fairly, regardless of race, politics or religion, and personal liking. They – and you – have tact and patience, and the reasonableness that makes others listen. They don't provoke trouble, but instead solve and settle other people's disputes. It is a rarity to hear of a violent criminal of 60. Children and adolescents sense the calm and safety and are drawn to older adults, who won't fly off the handle unpredictably, or snap: 'Can't you see I'm busy?'

It isn't that at our age we have nothing to do, but our priorities have shifted. A youngster needing to talk rates high, and the interruption of a mental or physical task counts lower than it did. People are important: Chapter 9 is all about relationships.

Of course, you won't suddenly feel calm and wise and in control in your changing world. Most likely it will be like teenageing all over again. You'll feel uncertain of yourself, what your role is and where you are heading. Some people react by worrying at the slightest thing.

Eleanor retired from her job before George. She found herself fussing and fretting over the house as she'd never done when she went to work. If George was five minutes late she would get into a state of anxiety and irritation, so that he dreaded coming home. Her mind settled into a happier routine when she began to help in the hospital shop and went to yoga. These activities got her out of the house, and brought her into contact with other people. In the autumn she's starting a course in china restoration, which will not only keep her busy, but provide her with worthwhile, saleable knowledge.

Other people, especially those living on their own, become cut off from others in their 60s and develop an exaggerated shyness. They may even begin to mistrust other human beings.

Desmond, whose marriage had ended in divorce, because he was never at home, had left himself short of interests and friends, outside his work. As a surgeon, he had no choice about retirement in his 60s. His unexpressed resentment at having what he loved taken away from him was directed at other people. He saw them all as enemies. Things were going from bad to worse when a former colleague asked for his help in producing a course on the history of medicine. Desmond took on the history of surgery. It involved time and study in the medical libraries and museums, and contact with the College. His enthusiasm was kindled and he found himself a competent lecturer, among historians, not the action men of surgery. He was lucky to be rescued by someone else.

'Nothing seems worthwhile any more': this thought is in the borderland of depression, affecting either sex. It's a draining away of purpose and pleasure: both common and natural before you've made your 60-plus life-plan and set it in motion. What is fatal is to delay until you 'feel like' tackling the situation. The worst thing you can do is to use alcohol to help you sleep or with the vague idea that it will make you feel better. Similarly, don't allow yourself to smoke more, or again, because 'what does it matter now'. Eating too much doesn't 'keep your strength up' but adds a burden to the system, while trying to crank-start your brain with too much tea and coffee has more effect on your kidneys.

These are the pitfalls. You have two safe and powerful resources to help you avoid them or get out of them: other people, those you know and those you can get to know, and the thousands of subjects of interest outside yourself.

Enjoy the fact that you are properly an adult at last. No-one else has the right to tell you what to do: you have the freedom and responsibility of running your own life, not, of course, forgetting your partner. Your other overriding responsibility is to check out the way ahead for all those behind you: your children and other people's. You have to show them that being 60-plus is nothing to fear. You are more, rather than less, of a person than before, and haven't you noticed that the later chapters of a book are usually more interesting than the first? All the time you are gaining a broader sense of values, greater understanding and tolerance and the knowledge that no experience in life is wasted. Every item helps you to grow psychologically towards being a fulfilled personality in a world full of wonders.

Chapter 4

PART I

Illness and what to do about it: Physical problems

'I enjoy convalescence. It is the part that makes the illness worthwhile.'

George Bernard Shaw

No-one goes through life without some experience of illness. Looking back, the illnesses which seemed so devastating at the time, with hindsight shrink to unimportant episodes. Any long-term disorders we've acquired on our journey, we've learned to live with by now.

We've safely passed through the age of susceptibility for some disorders. At this stage we are unlikely to develop rheumatoid arthritis, the common cold and such infections as tonsillitis, M.S. or the mysterious M.E., emphysema, Hodgkin's disease, and several aggressive forms of cancer. (Of course if, for instance, you already have one of these illnesses, hitting 60 won't cure it.) Our personalities will remain sensitive, outgoing etc., but we are less prone to the common neuroses: panics, agoraphobia, obsessional neurosis, anorexia.

Of course, we are not immune to accidents or the general run of illness, particularly the wear-and-tear type, like osteoarthritis or diverticular disease. Some illnesses result from a faulty lifestyle, which has continued for a considerable period. The good news is that it is never too late to lessen the effect by abandoning any bad habits now. The bonus is dramatic development in medical knowledge this last 50 years, providing new treatments and better guidelines on living.

Physical problems

The illnesses that are most feared include cancer, heart attack and stroke. All three can be avoided to some degree by a suitable diet and way of life, and all can be treated medically or surgically more effectively than ever before.

The illnesses which are the most likely to be troublesome to us are arthritis, diabetes and high blood pressure. Again, all of them are treatable, and the risk of developing them can be reduced to some extent.

Common physical symptoms and problems

ACCIDENTAL FALLS

Anyone can have a fall, but it is rather more likely after 60 than before. Between ages 65 and 69 around 30% of women and 13% of men will have a fall. A hard fall can hurt you and even crack a hip bone, but usually they merely shake you up. You feel so silly, especially as 90% of such tumbles are preventable. The slightly slower response of your circulation to changes of position, like getting up from a low chair, or to demands because of sudden extra effort, can make you feel dizzy and at risk of falling. You haven't allowed your blood pressure time to adjust.

Other factors that can cause your blood pressure to dip temporarily include alcohol, sleeping tablets, tranquillizers and antidepressants, water tablets and those for diabetes. Getting up in the night to pass water sometimes affects men similarly, by lowering the pressure.

You may have a weak joint, or your glasses may be wrong: get these checked if you've any doubts. But a third of falls are down to the environment: that is trailing wires, rucked-up rugs, a wet or polished floor like an ice-rink, uneven paving – and poor lighting, especially in an unfamiliar place at night. People with Parkinson's disease tend to shuffle when they walk, and must take particular care.

Although most falls have a simple, avoidable cause, exceptions are the mysterious 'drop attacks' which tend to affect mainly women, during pregnancy or at our age. Suddenly your legs give way, but almost as soon as they've let you down they are back to normal and you can get up. You don't feel ill or dizzy, only surprised. No-one knows the cause, but it is not connected with any illness: just a nuisance, not a worry. HRT may help.

Have a medical check IF:
- you have pain or difficulty in walking after a fall
- you have more than one fall
- you feel your eyes, sense of balance, joints or muscles may be at fault
- there is no reason to account for the fall.

FATIGUE AND WEAKNESS

Feeling tired all the time, a draining away of interest and energy, is particularly prevalent in the recently-retired. It is the excuse for ducking out of various activities until, in the end, no-one even suggests them. One thing is certain: this miserable condition is not something you should expect or accept after you turn 60 – or 70. Both American and British studies in 1990 found that while sex makes a difference (25% of women are affected, to 15% of men) age up to 80 has no effect on the proportion of people complaining of chronic fatigue.

The feeling is physical but the commonest causes are emotional, reflecting a sense of rejection, boredom and loneliness, with lack of purpose and anxiety about the future. (Frank depression is dealt with later.) There are a number of other conditions, less common, which may lead to this dreadful feebleness of body and spirit. Check:

- Are you on any medication? Beta-blockers, anti-epileptics, over-the-counter cold cures, regular laxatives, heavy use of vitamin pills, water tablets, 'tranqs' and 'sleepers', and antidepressants. Any of these may make you feel exhausted.
- Are you carrying a tiring load of overweight?
- Do you use alcohol to the detriment of your real nutrition?
- Do you smoke and so restrict the value of the air you breathe?
- Do you get a reasonable night's sleep? Six hours is enough, but do you have to get up several times to pass water, and is there noise or any other disturbing factor?

Could you have any of these disorders?

Anaemia, particularly if you are on an anti-epileptic, suffering from piles or hiatus hernia, take steroids or an anti-inflammatory drug for arthritis. Even if you don't look pale a blood test may show up anaemia – it occurs in nearly one in five women of our age. (Incidentally, you can look pale without anaemia.)

Diabetes: Have you been podgy over the years and are you

often thirsty, so that you have to drink and pass water more often than most people? A blood test will show up any diabetic tendency.

Hypothyroidism: Underactive thyroid gland. The signs are a general slow-down, constipation, increase in weight, loss of hair and a croaky voice. Again – a blood test gives the answer.

Deficiency states: For instance, of vitamins or minerals – sores at the corners of your mouth are an indication. Are you short of protein? If you can honestly say you have a good, mixed diet, deficiency is highly unlikely.

Chest or heart problems that make you short of breath can also make you feel tired.

Kidney and liver disorders can, similarly, lead to fatigue.

In general, serious illness shows up in more important symptoms than the common experience of feeling tired – which nine times out of ten is due to an unsatisfactory lifestyle.

SIDESTEPS

An exercise programme to keep your muscles, heart and lungs in top form – or to retrain them. Recent Russian and American work shows this approach is really effective.

   Mental stimulus: something different: do something new, go somewhere new, meet new people. Develop a new interest: you only need a library, radio and TV for this.

Pain in the chest

The commonest cause of pain in the chest is tension or anxiety. It is likely to be felt vaguely on the left side, and especially if you worry about your heart, it may go down your left arm. The medical causes of chest pain involve a range of conditions, some trivial, some important.

Angina: This pain is on the left side of the chest and all round it; it usually comes on when you are upset, or after exercise, and lasts only a few minutes. If it happens in the night, it means you've had an exciting dream – even if you don't remember it. Ordinarily the pain quickly subsides if you rest or suck a glyceryl trinitrate tablet (nitroglycerin) under your tongue. Sometimes thyroid problems, too much or too little, bring on angina.

The pain comes on when your heart speeds up, for any reason, and its muscle isn't getting enough blood. This is like any other muscle, for instance your calf muscles if you hurry upstairs.

SIDESTEPS

The ploy is gentle training, including after you have developed angina, as an adjunct to the tablets. It's simple: take a daily stroll, very gradually increasing its length. This opens up the smaller arteries to your heart muscle.

Overweight and anaemia need correcting.

TREATMENT

In mild cases a more peaceful lifestyle combined with graduated exercise is all that is necessary. GTN (glyceryl trinitrate) tablets are useful to have by you: see Chapter 5, page 108. If the angina becomes a real nuisance in your life, you will benefit from one of a range of medicines used for raised blood pressure (e.g. beta-blockers, verapamil, nifedipine). You need as low a dose as possible, since they all have some side-effects. At the crunch, you can choose by-pass surgery.

Myocardial infarction: This is the medical term for a coronary. It produces a pain like angina, but coming out of the blue, lasting half-an-hour or more, and making the victim feel sick and sweaty. Sometimes there is almost no chest pain. The best thing is to sit in a chair, rather than lie down, and send for the doctor – or an ambulance if it seems severe.

Pleurisy: Inflammation of the membrane covering the lung, causes a sharp, stabbing pain when you take a deep breath. It's like a stitch, only worse.

Inflammation of the gullet, with or without hiatus hernia, causes pain deep in the chest – associated with eating or taking an alcoholic drink.

Muscle strain can give you chest pain, for instance from coughing or unaccustomed exertion.

Shingles coming on causes chest pain on one side only. There's nothing to show, for the first day or two; then the rash appears.

If you suspect any of these medical causes of chest pain, have your doctor sort out what it is, and deal with it. You can expect an electrocardiogram or a chest X-ray among the investigations, but if there is no physical cause to be found, be glad, and consider tension (see page 87).

Shortness of breath

You probably can't run quite so fast to catch a bus, and although climbing stairs is first-rate exercise, it is likely that you will be puffed after three or four flights. You are perfectly well-equipped for ordinary living, but nature doesn't provide you with as much reserve capacity as earlier: in lung, heart and muscle power.

If you are noticeably and uncomfortably short of breath after minor effort, review your equipment.

Breathing apparatus: A hundred years ago infections were the commonest cause of illness and death in England. Think of the Brontes, and half-a-dozen of Dickens' characters. Today, with better food and hygiene, the slow decline of tobacco, and the magic of antibiotics and bronchodilators, the risks to the respiratory system (chronic bronchitis, asthma and lung cancer) are steadily reducing. Men still suffer more often than women, by nine to one.

Pumping apparatus: It can make you short of breath if you outrun your heart's reserve by exercise. You may feel your heart thumping hard, or have a choking sensation. An electrocardiogram will pinpoint any trouble in your heart.
   Some medicines, such as beta-blockers, steroids and most of the non-steroidal joint and muscle tablets cause retention of fluid. This gives your heart more to pump round.

Anaemia: If your blood is short in iron, it can't carry as much oxygen and your heart has to pump it round faster to supply the tissues — and it may feel the strain.

Overweight: This hampers your breathing, and there is a larger area that needs supplying with blood and oxygen.

SIDESTEPS

If you feel you are getting short of breath:

Don't smoke, and avoid smoky atmospheres.

Watch your weight.

Exercise gently to build up your reserves.

Walk tall: a slouch cramps your chest movement.

Don't go to bed in an ice-cold room after an evening in the warm.

Don't be a fresh-air fiend indoors. In winter, air your bedroom when you aren't in it, and never open windows when there's fog or mist about.

Take a few deep breaths morning and evening, to stretch the bottom 'corners' of your chest.

TREATMENT

Get your doctor to check you over. If he suggests medication, as well as an upgrade in lifestyle, be meticulous in taking it as directed. It is tempting, when you are feeling fine, to get slack about the very stuff that has made you better.

Swollen ankles

Puffy ankles are unsightly, feel tight and uncomfortable, and make poor circulation worse. The medical term is oedema: it is an accumulation of fluid that has oozed out of the tiniest blood vessels, the capillaries, into the tissues. In the ordinary way, blood is carried to the tissues in the thick, elastic-walled arteries to the network of capillaries, then back to the heart via the veins. While the flow through the arteries is driven by the heart, the return from the tissues occurs by gravity from the head, but by the massaging action of the muscles, in the limbs: when you move around. This is particularly important in the legs and feet, since gravity works the wrong way in this area.

The commonest type of ankle swelling is called postural or gravitational oedema. If you sit or stand around for long periods and seldom take brisk exercise, the back pressure will encourage seepage of fluid – especially if you have some varicose veins. This oedema develops during the day and subsides overnight, when you are horizontal. It is worse in hot weather.

No-one wears garters these days, but knee-highs, hold-ups and elasticated support panties and girdles – or a fat tummy – impede the blood flow into the upper parts of the leg veins, and increase the down pressure.

SIDESTEPS

Be considerate to your leg veins and capillaries.

Don't sit or stand for hours without using your muscles. If you are on a long flight, make the trip to the loo now and again, and use your calf muscles by ankle exercises while you are sitting.

Raise your feet slightly higher than your bottom whenever you can, for instance watching TV.

Watch your weight.

Avoid garments that impede the upward blood flow.

Support stockings may help, especially if you've a tendency to varicose veins.

Check your diet for too little protein, too much salt.

TREATMENT

All the sidesteps, plus cutting out extra salt, in cooking, sprinkled on or in very salty foods. Your doctor may prescribe, and should supervise your progress, with diuretic tablets. These help get rid of unwanted fluid by passing more water. Obviously the best time to take them is early in the day, when the effects are less inconvenient.

There are two snags: continued taking of diuretics is hard on your kidneys, and anyway they tend to lose their efficacy. At least have Sundays off.

Diuretics also tend to deplete your reserves of potassium: the natural sources are fruit, fresh or dried, fruit juices, potatoes, tomatoes, meat and dried peas.

It may be helpful to raise the foot of your bed a few inches.

Less likely causes of ankle swelling include:

Heart problems: If the heart is running the circulation less efficiently, fluid may accumulate and there will also be shortness of breath.

Thrombosis: The formation of a clot in a deep leg vein may interfere with the upward blood flow. A clot of this sort causes sudden pain and tenderness in the calf. This calls for medical advice, which will include resting up. Sometimes tiny clots form: they cause no pain, but may produce oedema: no special treatment is needed.

Poor nourishment, particularly in respect of proteins, in meat, fish, cheese, eggs, milk and beans, is an uncommon reason for oedema. In the Third World starving children have swollen abdomens. In the prosperous West adults may develop swelling of the ankles if their diet is deficient. They may be living on their own and not bothering, taking a drink instead of a meal, or be over-enthusiastic vegans.

High blood pressure

Normally blood pressure gradually increases with age from childhood upwards, peaking at around 83. In fact, if it doesn't go up you may be subject to dizzy spells because it is too low to keep an adequate blood flow to your brain. However, too high a pressure, especially in a sudden burst, can put a strain on the heart and blood vessels, which may be potentially dangerous. Those most at risk of a steep rise in blood pressure include the overweight, people who don't take much exercise, have an Afro-Caribbean heredity, or relatives with high pressure. The bonus for Afro-Caribbean men, and women of all races, is that even with raised blood pressure they are less likely than Caucasian men to have heart problems.

Because of the possible long-term dangers, and milder unpleasant symptoms in the short-term, it is worthwhile to deal with a tendency to high blood pressure. The milder problems are headaches, difficulties in concentration, tiredness and sometimes chest pain.

SIDESTEPS

For those likely to be vulnerable:

Keep your weight within 15% of the average (see pages 231–2).

Cut down on added salt and avoid bacon, ham, sardines, smoked fish, all tinned foods except fruit, brown sauce, pickles, soy sauce, and sandwich meats.

Stick to one alcoholic drink per sitting.

Give up smoking.

Regular aerobic exercise: For example, walking, but not weight training, nor the type that involves bursts of effort like squash or digging.

Keep your cool: Let the hassles of life pass you by like the hot air they mostly are. Philosophize.

Blood pressure is measured in two numbers: the higher, systolic value when the heart is actually pushing the blood round, and the lower, diastolic when it is relaxing between beats. A reading of 165/100 is a little too high and probably calls for treatment.

TREATMENT

The sidesteps above are part and parcel of high blood pressure treatment. Psychological relaxation is especially effective in the 'systolic' type of hypertension, likely in our age group.

There is a range of drugs useful in reducing blood pressure (systolic and diastolic). The first choice is usually a diuretic to increase the output of urine, which slightly lowers the volume of blood.

Beta-blockers are useful and make you feel calm, but they can cause a feeling of cold and lassitude, and tend to work best in younger people. (They can also lead to temporary impotence.) The more up-to-date medicines particularly suitable at our age are the calcium antagonists such as verapamil, and the ACE inhibitors such as captopril (see Chapter 5). Whichever medication is used the watchword of the treatment is gradual. A slow, gentle reduction of pressure is healthier than a dramatic drop: be patient if the tablets seem slow to work.

Diabetes mellitus

Diabetes has been known for thousands of years. Mellitus merely means sweet. It is on the increase all over the world, a pandemic. It comes in two main types. The more severe comes on early in life, affecting more boys than girls – and continuing through life. The second variety is commoner and usually comes on after 50, but especially between 60 and 70. It tends to run in families and to affect those with a sweet tooth, who have been plump for some years.

The body begins to lose control of its carbohydrate metabolism in particular: that is, it doesn't deal effectively with starchy and sugary foods, like bread, potatoes, pasta, cakes and sweets. The pancreas, a sliver of gland near the stomach, may not produce enough insulin – but equally important, the tissues become less responsive to it, as though the mechanism had become worn.

Diabetes is troublesome, not so much for its characteristic symptoms of thirst, drinking excessively and passing a lot of water, but for its complications. It can upset every system of the body and – most dangerously – increase the risks of stroke or heart attack. It can damage your sight seriously, impair your bladder and bowel function, and make chest, skin and urinary infections more likely. An annoying symptom is itching where the skin comes into contact with urine.

All-in-all it makes good sense to take some precautions against developing diabetes, especially if other relatives have had it. If it does creep up, it is important to take the medical advice seriously.

SIDESTEPS

Eating: Correct any excess weight. Watch your sweet tooth and try to train your tastes towards proteins, vegetables and salads.

Exercise: Walking or whatever you enjoy helps the tissues to keep or regain their sensitivity to insulin.

TREATMENT

Diet is essential: say 1000 kilocalories a day (of which only a tenth is carbohydrate) is often enough to control early diabetes. Medicines may also be necessary to keep the sugar level in your blood down to a healthy level. The safest are the short-acting types, such as tolbutamide or glipizide. Very few diabetics with onset in our age group require insulin injections, but you need to get into the habit of checking your water for excess sugar, with a simple kit.

Diabetics must take particular care of their feet. The circulation is often poor, so they need warmth as well as meticulous hygiene. Chilblains or injuries easily become infected and are slow to heal.

Back pain

Back pain is common, wearing and depressing. The agonizing problems of a slipped disc, which can cause a strong young adult to lie flat for a fortnight, are unlikely to affect you. You – or I – are more liable to a nagging ache, which doesn't clear up in two weeks. The likeliest causes are the wear and tear of osteoarthritis, or osteoporosis.

Osteoporosis: Our bones become lighter and less solid from around 25, but noticeably so after 40. If the process goes too far or too fast it results in a fragile bone structure – osteoporosis. The bones in the back may get squashed out of shape, especially if they have an extra heavy body to carry. Mild aching may suddenly change to sharp pain, often after lifting something weighty: one of the vertebrae has given under the strain. This usually takes four or five weeks to heal, but if several vertebrae (the small bones that make up the spine) are affected you may notice that you've lost a little height.

The causes of osteoporosis are unclear, but thyroid problems predispose to it, also diabetes, rheumatoid arthritis or having to take steroid medicines. It tends, among women, to run in the family, with white and Asian races more vulnerable than black. It occurs much more frequently in women than men, and especially those who went through the change early and did not have hormone replacement therapy (HRT). Violeta Chamorro, President of Nicaragua is a sufferer – and very glamorous.

Men are more or less immune unless they drink heavily, when they can develop it any time after 30.

SIDESTEPS

Regular exercise – most important of all.

Don't get fat.

Eat dairy products for natural calcium and vitamin D: cheese, yogurt, milk (including skimmed). Eat oranges for vitamin C.

Cut down alcohol, tea, coffee.

Cut out smoking.

HRT: With your doctor's approval, at any age, for women.

TREATMENT

Use all the sidestep manoeuvres – including exercise as soon as you can manage it. Don't rest up with your back pain for more than a few days, nor wear a supportive corset for more than a week at a time: either of these makes matters worse long-term. There are various medicines being tried out for osteoporosis. HRT is both a preventive and a remedy, in women. Etidronate is also useful for women of our age, and for men: it is non-hormonal. Calcium tablets used to be popular but have been shown not to help, and unless you are prescribed a specific dose by your doctor for a specific reason, don't take synthetic vitamin D. A build-up of this vitamin can lead to general weakness and fatigue, headache, vomiting and diarrhoea, and the laying down of calcium in your arteries, heart and kidneys – not your bones. See Appendix, pages 218–19.

Osteoarthritis: You are sure to have some signs of this. Everyone does, in that it is a general reaction of the joints to being used. After years of service the cartilage lining in a joint can become slightly roughened, and the bones bordering on it grow rather untidily. Sometimes you can hear the untidy bits grating, for instance in your neck, if you move your head from side to side. The muscles nearby may be irritated by the bone. We are usually quite unaware, until overgrown bits of bone get in the way of full movement, and annoy the muscles, causing pain.

By age 35 the lower back shows these signs of use-reaction in 60% of men, 44% of women, if examined by X-ray. Osteoarthritis occurs all over the body, but it is likely to be most noticeable in the hip (see below) or back. The effects are stiffness and backache, often developing overnight. The stiffness wears off within half-an-hour of your getting moving, but the discomfort may lurk on.

The changes of osteoarthritis are so commonplace as to be part of normality. Factors which make them worse include injuries, operations on your bones and joints, and overuse from athleticism. Men have more trouble with osteoarthritis of the back than women, probably because of more physical activity. Obesity is also a risk factor, including inexplicably for osteoarthritis of the finger joints.

SIDESTEPS

Don't overwork your joint/muscle system. You'll know next day, if you do. Overweight means overwork, too.

Keep all moving parts moving by gentle stretching exercises every day.

TREATMENT

If you are going through a painful period with your back, the most effective medicines are the non-steroidal anti-inflammatory group (NSAIDs), such as ibuprofen and

piroxicam. You must take these with or after food, as they
may irritate your stomach. For this reason, and also
because they have no actual curative effect, do not
continue on these drugs for more than a week or two at
a time. See Chapter 5, page 111.

The other limb of treatment is physiotherapy,
including, if you are lucky, hydrotherapy – exercises in
lovely warm water. You can do a lot off your own bat by
starting the day with a hot bath and then doing exercises.
The first one is to sit slumped in a hard chair and then
straighten up to your full, sitting height: repeat three or
four times. You can work up to other exercises from there.

A firm mattress is always recommended, but any
change in your bed is likely to make matters worse until
your body gets used to it.

Osteomalacia is cousin to osteoporosis, but less common.
Nevertheless it also affects our age group, and women
especially. It is a weakening of the bones due to deficiency
of vitamin D: the one you manufacture in your skin when
it is exposed to the sunlight. It's perhaps not surprising
that ladies in misty Scotland are particularly susceptible
towards the end of winter. A dark complexion is an added
disadvantage. The symptoms are discomfort rather than
back pain, tenderness of all the bones, and climbing the
stairs seems especially hard work.

SIDESTEPS

Make the most of any winter sunshine, and include butter
or margarine fortified with vitamin D in your diet. Take
particular care if you are on an anti-epileptic medicine, as
this may interfere with absorption of the vitamin, but
don't take any concentrated vitamin preparations
without your doctor's say-so.

TREATMENT

Your doctor may want to give you a calciferol injection or high-dose vitamin D tablets for two or three months. It is dangerous to go on with these indefinitely. Meanwhile, review your diet and the time you spend outdoors.

Paget's disease: Osteoporosis is the top bone problem, but Paget's affects up to 10% of those between 45 and 75. It occurs slightly more often in men, and among those brought up in a 'doggy' family. There is a mild hereditary link, too. The bones slowly grow too thick. Those most often affected are the pelvis, backbone, thigh and skull.

There are usually no symptoms apart from the bone changing shape and the overlying skin feeling warm, but in a few unfortunates the bones, including the back, ache, particularly in the night.

SIDESTEPS

None.

TREATMENT

Rest and ordinary pain-killer or anti-inflammatories (NSAIDs) help a little, but if the pain is troublesome your doctor can prescribe specific treatment: calcitonin by injection or etidronate tablets.

Other causes of back pain: Persistent bad posture (remember your back both looks and feels better straight) and depression. If you feel you have the cares of the world on your shoulders, your back may ache in sympathy.

Painful hips and knees

Osteoarthritis: Pain in one or both hips is almost always due to this, and like the wrist or back, affects men more often than women, especially between 59 and 64. In women more joints are likely to be involved, particularly hands, knees and feet. An arthritic knee will be out-of-shape, and will grate when you move it, and the hip will become increasingly stiff – and, of course, painful.

SIDESTEPS

The same as for osteoarthritis in the back, including HRT for women.

TREATMENT

This, too, is similar except that with intractable problems replacement surgery is possible. Hip replacement is a standard operation today. If you work well at the post-op exercises you can expect to be a new woman or man within three weeks. The only snag is that the artificial joint begins to wear out in about 15 years, and a repeat is not usually as successful. This is one small advantage if you have to delay your first operation because of waiting lists.

Knee replacement is also becoming established for severe cases, but there are fewer surgeons with much experience, so you need to go to a major centre for this operation.

Rheumatoid arthritis: This affects women three times as often as men, and usually starts before age 60. In our age group it is usually a continuation of an ongoing disorder: the give-away is the swelling and distortion of the joints of the hand.

SIDESTEPS

Watch your diet: Not a matter of vitamin tablets, but real food: protein in meat, fish, cheese, eggs; iron in sardines; All-bran; chocolate; vitamin C in oranges and salads.

TREATMENT

Useful medication includes salicylates, NSAIDs, penicillamine (and, in severe cases, methotrexate). Physiotherapy is particularly valuable; and surgery for some.

Feet: Hammer toes and bunions can make walking a misery, and are often a legacy from rheumatoid arthritis. The only cure is surgery, but meanwhile chiropody helps – and shoes which are kind to their occupants.

Unrecognized fracture: Occasionally when someone complains of a painful hip interfering with walking, a tiny crack is found in the thigh bone, near the hip joint. The injury may have been no more than jarring, especially in a woman with osteoporosis, and ignored as of no account. X-ray reveals the diagnosis. Treatment is orthopaedic, and varies.

Digestive system problems

This remarkable system normally continues indefinitely its wonderful work of taking in and processing food to repair and fuel the tissues, and also discarding the waste. Most of the possible snags are either avoidable or you can deal with them yourself.

Indigestion: This is likelier in men.

SIDESTEPS

Greater moderation in the use of alcohol, coffee, tea and chocolates. Cultivate calm.

TREATMENT

If you develop an ulcer there are almost magical tablets: cimetidine and ranitidine. Old-fashioned antacids and milky foods are no help, we now know.

Hiatus Hernia: A leakage backwards up the swallowing tube of part-digested food from the stomach causes burning discomfort, especially if you have a late, large dinner and then lie down in bed.

SIDESTEPS

Have a reasonable gap between dinner and bedtime. Foods that cause most trouble are coffee, citrus fruits, and chocolate plus alcohol and cigarettes. Cut them out in the evening.

Constipation: 25% of 70-year-olds in the United States and Britain regularly take laxatives. You don't need to be one of them. The automatic muscles of the colon do not lose their strength, although the external muscles do.

SIDESTEPS

Foster the gastro-colic reflex: after the night's fasting, if hot food and fluid arrive in the stomach in reasonable quantity, a message is flashed down to the lower reaches of the gut, reminding them to shove any waste matter along towards the exit. After breakfast is the most physiological time to empty the bowels.

Avoid such constipating drugs as codeine, antidepressants or aluminium hydroxide indigestion medicine.

Have a good, hot, bulky breakfast: porridge is excellent, with plenty of hot drink. In general go for whole-grain cereals, bran, citrus fruits, plums and bananas, oatcakes, jacket potatoes, green vegetables – and plenty of water. Be sparing with white bread, cakes, pastry, pasta, rice. Keep up your general muscle tone with tummy exercises.

TREATMENT

Train your bowel with reducing doses of a bulk laxative, for instance containing ispaghula, or lactulose. Get into a regular routine and expect the training to take months.

Change in bowel habit: If it persists over two or three weeks – have your doctor check out possible causes. (At the worst, bowel cancer is among the easiest to cure – and a high fibre diet is good protection against it.)

Trouble with the water

The embarrassing problem of lapses in control affects 5% of adolescents and 15% of 60-year-olds.

'Stress incontinence' can catch you out at any age. You laugh, or you feel an urgent need to pass water when you've almost reached the loo – and a leakage occurs. There is another type, often coinciding, when a little water escapes when there's no special pressure or a desire 'to go'. It is as though the sphincter of the bladder 'forgets' now and again to keep tightly closed.

Alcohol, too much tea or coffee, sleeping tablets, tranquillizers and, of course, water tablets can all interfere with control. Women who have had babies are more at risk, and the pressure on the bladder of excess fat adds to the problem in either sex.

Urinary infections, commoner in women, are a frequent cause of control difficulties. The best avoiding action is to take plenty of fluids to flush the system through. Your doctor will supply antibiotics if you develop an infection, and may suggest your taking a small dose regularly as a preventive.

Prostate problems: The prostate gland, situated by the neck of the bladder, undergoes a normal, harmless enlargement from 50 onwards in men – and also pet dogs. It can be a nuisance in some men, by interfering with the outflow of urine. The best answer is removal of the unwanted tissue by a safe minor operation nowadays: the results are 88% successful. If for some reason you can't have surgery, there is a range of drugs which help.

You can suspect your prostate if you find you've lost power in your flow of urine, and you can also develop a dribbling leak.

Management of poor control: Have your doctor check for treatable medical causes, review your medicines and lifestyle, and practise bladder control. Do this by deliberately stopping and starting every time you pass water. Sphincter exercises for women, run by nurses, are available in many health centres and doctors' surgeries, and at hospitals. Not everyone is successful with exercises, so thank goodness it is so easy and discreet to feel secure by wearing pantipads or sanipads.

Seeing and hearing

Communication is the essence of human existence and never more so than now. It depends on sight and hearing. Any impairment is a major work, social and safety disadvantage. It would be extraordinary if no adjustment or assistance were required in these two key senses by this time. You wouldn't expect your car to run for over 50 years without servicing, so have a sight and hearing check now. In both areas technological advances have introduced treatments undreamed of when we were born.

The reduction in elasticity which crops up in various parts of the body, noticeably in the skin, also affects the hearing and seeing apparatus.

EYES

Presbyopia: A mild loss of flexibility in the lens of your eye makes it more difficult for the small ciliary muscles to pull it into a different shape for you to focus on close work – like reading this. At rest, the eye is focused for distant vision, but from about 45 onwards you may notice it becoming more comfortable to hold your book at a distance. (For short-sighted people this is a bonus.)

Presbyopia is the term for this normal development. Reading glasses are the simple answer.

Cataract: Everyone develops cataracts (hard areas in the lens) but most of us are unaware. For the minority whose sight is affected first-class help is at hand: a neat transplant operation as a day case. Most people don't need glasses afterwards.

Retinal damage: This does not occur through age, but may develop with diabetes, high blood pressure, and some kidney disorders: laser treatment is excellent.

Dark adaptation: A different set of retinal cells come into operation in the dark. Since now your body tends to run everything in a more leisurely fashion, it will take a little longer for your eyes to adapt to a change of light. Allow for this (it's only a minute or so) if you are a motorist.

Irritable eyes: Because you make slightly less tear fluid nowadays, your eyes may feel dry and uncomfortable, especially when you wake up, yet water too much at other times. The answer is to use 'artificial tears'. The important ingredient is hypromellose. You cannot use them with soft contact lenses.

Damage to the optic nerve: This is the pathway that carries information from your retina to your brain. It can be poisoned by various substances: alcohol, particularly meths, tobacco, some insecticides, quinine, and excessive use of steroids. Moderation is the watchword, for your sight's sake.

EARS

Loss of flexibility affects the middle and inner parts of the ear, making it more difficult to hear high-pitched sounds. We lose the ability to hear the squeak of a bat during our 30s, and some of us in our 60s or later have difficulty in catching the beginnings and ends of words, especially involving t, d, s or p. This explains the stereotype who says: 'Don't mumble', and then complains: 'Don't shout!' He can hear the vowel sounds at full volume.

A hearing test will establish whether and which part of your hearing is less sharp. From that a tailor-made aid can be made. Modern aids are tiny and neat, and run on tiny, cheap batteries. They can revolutionize your family and social life.

Damage to the ears from excessive noise (it used to be gunners, now it's more often loud music) can overstrain the listening apparatus, causing deafness and also the annoying whistling sound, tinnitus. It can be helped by masking.

Stroke

This is not a common problem, but the thought of it may be worrying. It is largely avoidable, and already the risk has been reduced by 20% in the UK and 32% in the US. The medical term for a stroke is cerebral vascular accident (CVA). It comprises a sudden loss in blood supply to a part of the brain, causing weakness and loss of sensation, say, in one arm, or unconsciousness. If it only lasts a few hours it is called a transient ischaemic attack (TIA), which is a useful warning to take care.

Risk factors: Age over 85, male sex, being Chinese, Japanese or black American. You can't change these but they are reminders to take avoiding action. If you have heart, blood pressure or diabetic problems, get your doctor's advice and co-operate. The other risk factors are under your personal control:

- too much fatty food,
- alcoholic binges,
- cigarettes,
- lack of exercise,
- poor intake of fruit and vegetables,
- overweight: especially the type, commoner in men, in which the waist is wider than the hips.

If several risk factors apply to you it is worth doing what US businessmen have been doing for years. Take a 300 mg aspirin tablet and a 50 mg vitamin C tablet daily after food. These make clotting of the blood less likely.

Recovery from a stroke: Strokes are notorious for leaving the sufferer feeling depressed, irritable and easily upset. If the mood aspect becomes a nuisance, your doctor can help with a short course of an antidepressant. Otherwise, after the acute illness you've a busy time ahead with the rehab programme, whether it's you or your partner. Improvement continues over a whole year – so the important principle is persistence. If one area of the brain has been damaged, other parts can learn to take over, with time and patience: as happened with Pasteur.

Cancer

No disorder is desirable, but the least popular is cancer. The good news is:

- Three-quarters of cancers are already curable, and research is advancing steadily.
- Nearly all lung cancers are avoidable, and it is still worthwhile to give up smoking at 60-plus.
- The antioestrogen, tamoxifen, reduces the risk of breast cancer in vulnerable people.
- Mammograms give even earlier warning of breast cancer.
- Cervical cancer can be zapped before it has begun, through smear and newer screening tests.
- Moderating alcohol intake reduces the risk of cancer of the throat, liver and gullet.

The right diet helps to cut the risk of cancer, according to the 1991 Committee on the Medical Aspects of Food. Researchers believe that dietary faults are responsible for 30% of the risk – but they aren't sure how. They recommend, pro tem:

- Bread (wholemeal and white): twice as much as now.
- Vegetables: twice as much.
- Fruit: half as much again.
- Potatoes: slightly more.
- Meat: same amount, but leaner.
- Milk: same amount but semi-skimmed.
- Spreads: same amount but low-fat type.
- Chocolate, jam, sugar: half the amount.
- Soft drinks, biscuits, cakes, puddings: half.
- Crisps, chips: half quantity, reduced fat.

Protein: You need adequate amounts to keep your immune system healthy. It checks rogue cells that could form cancers as well as dealing with infection.

Vitamins: Particularly relevant to cancer prevention are beta-carotene and vitamins C and E. For preference, rely on natural sources. Beta-carotene: carrots, tomatoes, apricots, bananas, red and yellow sweet potatoes, oranges. Vitamin C: fresh fruit, especially oranges and blackcurrants, salads. Vitamin E: wheat germ and other vegetable oils, coconuts, eggs, soya, corn, peanuts, cereals.

Chapter 4

PART II

Illness and what to do about it: Psychological problems

'Hope not sunshine every hour,
Fear not clouds will always lower.
Happiness is but a name,
Make content and ease thy aim.'

Robert Burns

The great disadvantage of psychological suffering is that it doesn't show, and hasn't an impressive medical name. It is more distressing than a physical illness, but the amount of sympathy you get is much less. You may even come to think it's your fault, that you are weak and a failure.

'Nothing seems worthwhile any more'

This is the keynote of DEPRESSION, the commonest emotional disorder at any age. Apart from all enjoyment draining out of your life, you lose energy, concentration, sleep and appetite. It is an illness. The causes may be physical: the aftermath of a viral illness like influenza, or a painful one like arthritis. Or it can be set off by some medicine the doctor has prescribed, such as an antibiotic, a sleeping tablet, a tranquillizer or a steroid.

The likeliest cause, however, lies in what's happened in your life lately. Some events are obviously depressing: such as bereavement or the threat of it, children moving miles away, development of a serious illness in a family member, or financial disaster. About three-quarters of cases of depression follow some adverse event. Anything that requires a rethink and adjustment throws a strain on you. Moving house, leaving or changing a job, becoming a grandparent: everything has an impact. Depression may be secondary to worry – about money, your health, your grown-up children.

SIDESTEPS

The best preventive of depression, particularly for men, surprisingly, is to have someone close in whom to confide. Understanding between you and your partner or your best friend is worth working for. Talking about problems and feelings – honestly – with someone you trust takes the sting out.

Another ploy is to stagger those important events in your life, over which you have control. If you have to retire in April don't consider moving house or a cruise around the world until several months later. Bunching life-events together risks giving your mind too much to take on board at any one time: just as you can't climb a mountain, sing an aria and work out your income tax simultaneously.

If you suffer the loss of someone important to you, don't wait to develop a depression: get bereavement counselling straightaway. Other losses which might seem less significant, for instance of a pet or a voluntary job, can also throw you.

TREATMENT

Your doctor's help may be vital: for full discussion and perhaps medication.

To help yourself you must seek company – although it may be the last thing you feel like. Any human company is better than none. Exercise is beneficial – even if it's an effort.

Alcohol, going to bed early, or taking a holiday makes matters worse. Planning a holiday for when you are better is fine, and rearranging the furniture is a useful mental and physical exercise. Walnuts and bananas provide the raw materials for making your own spirit-raising chemicals.

'I've got no confidence'

This feeling may be part of depression or anxiety as a common reaction to being 60-plus. We can easily be made to feel that we are of no importance now – by other people's attitudes, life changes which rob us of our accustomed roles, and less money.

SIDESTEPS AND TREATMENT

Confidence-raising exercise: Every morning write down one thing that you are going to do in the day that will be beneficial to *you*. It may be mundane, like reorganizing your desk drawer, luxurious like having a hair-do, social like keeping a friendship in repair even with a 'phone call, healthy like a brisk walk, stimulating like visiting a gallery or anything that pleases, amuses or satisfies you, or relaxes you. At the end of the day, tick off that you've done it. Follow the exercise for a fortnight. You mustn't miss a day, and you mustn't repeat yourself.

'I'm a worrier'

A chronic state of anxiety also involves lack of self-confidence. It can involve anything and everything, but is particularly likely to be centred on your health. Unfortunately, worry itself is likely to produce such symptoms as headache, stiff neck or shoulder, indigestion and flatulence, palpitations and chest pain, poor sleep and fatigue.

SIDESTEPS

Have a medical check every five years or so, preferably one of those run by a medical insurance agency. Pay for it and believe it. Follow any advice.

Symptom-dating: When, as is inevitable, you develop a symptom, such as a pain or a cough, mark a date in your diary six weeks ahead. The chances are, that when you come to review the situation then, whatever was wrong will have improved, through time, the greatest healer. If it hasn't, it is now reasonable to consult your doctor for reassurance or advice.

Another type of anxiety is, you realize, silly. You can become nervous about travelling, or shopping, or feel tormented in case you've left the front door open or the fire on.

SIDESTEPS AND TREATMENT

Stamp on fears from the first moment they enter your mind – by doing whatever you feel apprehensive about, as soon as possible and several times. Involve a companion if you must.

Nip in the bud the checking tendency. Determine to check only once, ever.

Make yourself busy outside your home for all forms of worrying.

Company: spend time with other people, but unlike in depression, don't talk about yourself or your worries. It wears your friends out.

'I feel I need it'

We may not be in the age range for heroin, crack or 'E', but we are certainly the likeliest to have developed a mild dependence on some perfectly legal chemical. The trouble is that, just as with a narcotic, your body adapts its metabolism to any chemical it is exposed to regularly, and – temporarily – works less well without it.

Another problem is that your liver and kidneys, while more than adequate for dealing with normal food and drink, are not so quick at detoxifying and clearing the body of other chemicals, like medicines and alcohol, as they were ten years ago. This means that the same intake as always can now be a damaging excess: particularly important if you are taking a substance often or regularly.

Chemicals that can do harm may be obtained socially: alcohol, tobacco; bought over the counter: pain-killers, cold cures, indigestion tablets, anti-diarrhoea tablets, cough medicines, nerve or mood tablets (the so-called herbal types); and those prescribed by your doctor: sleeping tablets, tranquillizers, some antidepressants, and the more powerful pain-killers and cough medicines.

They all do harm if used persistently over a long period. This does not mean the medicines you need for a physical or psychological illness. Sleepers and tranquillizers interfere with memory; pain-killers affect the liver and kidneys, and sometimes the stomach; common anti-diarrhoeals contain morphine; cough medicines can upset the emotional balance; and cold cures often contain alcohol as well as chemicals that can disrupt the whole autonomic nervous system. Long-continued use of laxatives is a special case: overstimulating the colon is like flogging a tired horse. In the end it can no longer respond, and the natural reflex is lost.

ALCOHOL

Alcohol is in a class of its own. Most people enjoy a drink. To 'need' alcohol to unwind or to get to sleep or enjoy a social event, is bad news. It harms your stomach lining, worsens hiatus hernia, raises your blood pressure unpredictably, and damages your brain cells. No matter how it makes you feel at the time, alcohol is a depressant over a 24-hour period.

We all know the gross damage socially, intellectually and physically caused by heavy use of alcohol, often to some of the nicest people. There are two age-peaks for serious alcoholic damage: 45–55 and 65–75. Men are more often victims than women, but the latter are catching up fast, especially in the older age group. They are often less obvious.

SIDESTEPS

With tobacco, the only way is to stop, but with alcohol it is strict moderation. Always have two alcohol-free days in the week, and no more than two or three drinks on any one day. There is no benefit in keeping off spirits in favour of wine or lager. Sherry is probably the most generally damaging drink if used too much.

'You can't trust anyone these days'

If you find this bleak thought crossing your mind frequently it is likely that you are suffering from a depression or an anxiety state, and may need your doctor's help.

SIDESTEPS

If you spend a lot of time alone these days, or are becoming slightly hard of hearing you need to obtain and get used to an adequate and comfortable hearing aid, and modify your lifestyle. Sometimes the Church can provide a gentle way into becoming a part of the community again. It is so easy to slip into isolation without realizing, and let the extravert side of your nature shrivel up.

'I'd give anything for a good night's sleep'

Sleep is rather like the Christmasses and summer holidays of our childhood. We remember it as better than it was: 'sleeping like a log', long hours of dreamless slumber, asleep 'as soon as my head touched the pillow'. Nightmares and sleep destroyed by examination and boyfriend or girlfriend anxieties occur mainly in youthful sleep, but we forget. True, we sleep less heavily as older adults; and women more than men may feel dissatisfied with its quality. There is no health risk in this, however, since if the body and brain actually need sleep they will impose it on you willy-nilly.

SIDESTEPS

Never have a doze in the day. You used not to when you were sleeping so well. Risk times are after lunch or when you are watching TV in the evening. Don't go to bed at nursery time: keep your intellectual interests alive or go in for more social activity. At the other end of the night, don't get up later just because you may not have to get to a paid job on time. Sleep won't fill in the gaps if you leave your life too empty. It's your responsibility. You may have been expecting to enjoy just sitting back, resting – only to find it soon gets boring. You are as alive now as when you were 40.

TREATMENT

Develop a relaxing, winding-down ritual. A hot bath before bed is relaxing, and a hot milky drink a proven way to encourage peaceful sleep. Alcoholic nightcaps unfortunately tend to make your sleep restless in the second half of the night, and stimulate the kidneys to produce urine. The setting should be a comfortable bed, a room neither stuffy nor cold, and a book, radio or TV to switch your mind off. Hypnotics from your doctor inevitably lose their efficacy over about two months, but your sleep is even worse – at first – when you try to give them up. It's a matter of persisting for a fortnight or so, but worthwhile.

It is the longer term side-effects of 'sleepers' that are so undesirable: memory and learning powers are insidiously dulled. Many unfortunates have been thought to have Alzheimer's or some other degenerative brain disorder – when all that was happening was hypnotic build-up.

If you have to suffer some nights with poor sleep, at least have the company of all-night radio. Choose talk, not music, and use one tiny earphone to avoid disturbing your sleeping partner. Don't get up and range around, read or make a drink: such activities are apt to wake you up. Most of all, don't stay in bed later if you've had a bad night, nor go to bed earlier than usual the next night. What is required is a habit, as unchanging as possible, especially the timing.

'I've got another of my headaches'

Everyone has a headache now and again. If you are plagued by them, look to your lifestyle.

Skipping a meal, or too long a gap, can lead to low blood sugar: the immediate cure is a biscuit and a banana or a handful of raisins. Have regular meals from now on, and betweens if necessary. Women are more vulnerable than men.

Lack of fluid: Have a drink, but not the alcoholic variety which will only make matters worse. Increase your daily intake of water-based drinks, especially when it's hot or you are rushing around.

Alcohol, especially red wine, sherry, port or beer, has a chemical effect as well as a dehydrating effect. Try sticking to champagne, and drink plenty of water.

Cheese: Stilton and mature hard cheeses, like red wine, contain tyramine. This can cause migraine in migraine sufferers and headache in anyone, particularly in the late evening.

Chocolate and citrus fruits contain certain other amines and can cause headaches in the susceptible.

Caffeine: Strong filter coffee is far likelier than instant, or tea, to give you a headache.

Chinese meals and others containing monosodium glutamate may cause a headache – look on the labels of foods you cook at home.

Other factors: Ice-cream or any very cold food, too hot a room, a smoky atmosphere, lack of sleep – and most of all tension – also cause headaches.

TREATMENT

Take aspirin or paracetamol without delay (it's easier to get rid of a headache at the beginning) and wash your face in cool water. For the future check your eating etc., and re-read the section on worry. Discuss with your doctor if the headaches continue: there are some magical new medicines for genuine migraine.

Alzheimer's disease

This is included because so many people worry about it – unnecessarily. If you are reading this there is no way you could have the disorder – but an older relative might possibly develop it. The chief victim is the responsible relative who finds that someone they know and love is gradually losing touch with them mentally (see Chapter 10).

SIDESTEPS

There is massive research into this problem because of the increase in the number of people in the at-risk age groups, mainly 85-plus. There are several leads, but so far the only reasonable avoidables are excessive use of medicines containing aluminium (some antacids) and long boiling of foods in uncoated aluminium saucepans. Alcohol, hypnotics and minor tranquillizers – to excess – make matters worse but do not cause Alzheimer's.

TREATMENT

A cure is still out-of-sight, but a stimulating environment with other people around probably delays the progress of the disorder. The major concern is not to overload the caring person.

Losses

The most devastating loss is the death of your partner, or even the diagnosis of a life-threatening disease (see Chapters 9 and 12). There is a major rehearsal with your parents, usually (see Chapter 10). Other losses that can throw you are the emigration, permanently, of a child; serious loss of financial or other status, or a threat to your own health; or the death of a pet around which you'd built your daily routine.

The normal response to bereavement starts with a feeling of unreality, as though it couldn't be happening to you. You are thirsty but you can't eat. Sooner or later you are caught up in a confusing muddle of emotions: anxiety, guilt, anger and pangs of grief. You can't settle to anything at first and you may feel the dead person close to you: this is comforting. All this is to be expected and, in the ordinary way, gradually subsides as you make adjustments. A few people, often those who were super-brave, react badly and develop a depression or physical symptoms. Men, in particular, are susceptible to the latter, including muscle and joint pains, chest pains and palpitations, or shortness of breath. They can even become ill.

SIDESTEPS

If you have been through any life-event that entails a loss or disrupts the way you run your life, it is urgent to take preventive action. This amounts to talking – to doctors, counsellors, friends, other relatives or anyone you know until you've taken the sting out of your sadness, and can cope with it. No tablets, either for sleeping or anti-depressant, will help. They only delay your getting over it. The same goes for holidays: it's worse when you return. Save up your holiday for the time when it will really do you good.

TREATMENT

Grief after loss is normal and natural; only if you develop physical symptoms do you require any treatment from your doctor, apart from a sympathetic ear and reassurance.

Chapter 5

Doctors and medicines

'I do not want two diseases, one nature-made,
one doctor-made.'

Napoleon Bonaparte, 1820

Napoleon was obviously on to the idea of side-effects, the
snag which accompanies much medical treatment. Yet
there's no-one who hasn't taken some medicine from
time to time, and very few who don't have occasion to
consult their doctor sometimes. In any case, it is more
comfortable for both parties if you and your family doctor
are at least acquainted, and you may feel like old friends
if there has been a long involvement.

Most problems that crop up in your body, and minor
emotional upsets are best first dealt with by your doctor
who will have expertise in all the common ailments. He
is also well-placed to decide when and which type of
specialist help you may need, and to brief the consultant
about your medical history and situation.

The consultation with the family doctor

Practices are run in many and diverse ways: one of the
most modern and highly-organized I know is in a small

country village. Some have efficient practice-managers and smooth-running appointments systems, while others operate on a more flexible, ad hoc basis. Whichever style, to get the best out of it, apply the guidelines:

In an EMERGENCY, tell the receptionist, using this word, immediately you get through. Say why in one sentence, then give your name, address and telephone number. If the doctor isn't going to be available promptly, consider calling an ambulance to take the invalid to an Accident and Emergency Department. While you wait – for doctor or ambulance – get the sequence of events clear in your mind, and preferably write them down. Get together all the medicines the person, you or whoever is ill, has been taking.

Apart from emergencies:

1. Don't delay making an appointment, or asking for a house call, from foolish stoicism, pride – or fear.
2. If at all possible, try to call early in the day, and early in the week. The doctor's nightmare is that all his patients in trouble will struggle on through the week, until Friday evening or dawn on Sunday, before admitting that they need help.
3. Before you telephone, for yourself or someone else, plan what you are going to say: the reason for worrying, the degree of urgency, any medication being taken, whether a surgery or home visit is required, and, as a reminder, any ongoing disorder, such as diabetes or emphysema.
4. Wherever you see the doctor, have at hand the containers of any medicines you are taking, both prescribed and over-the-counter. He can check the dosage etc.
5. Make a note of three or four questions you might forget to ask the doctor. It isn't sensible to make a

longer list, because you won't remember all the answers anyway.

6. Tell or remind the doctor about any drugs that didn't suit you in the past, because of allergy or sensitivity, and any that have been particularly helpful.

7. Mention any important changes or events in your personal life. Include the good as well as the bad happenings, for instance becoming a grandparent, facing retirement, moving house.

8. IF YOU'VE THE SLIGHTEST DOUBT about what the doctor meant, or over any instructions, say so at once. Don't hope to work it out afterwards. I've known people to take stimulants at bedtime and muscle-relaxants before a day's work, because they weren't clear. Check with the doctor and check the labels from the pharmacy to be double-sure.

Seeing a specialist

Why see a specialist? You don't have to have a serious illness to see a specialist. You may ask to see one since this is your right – but more often it will be your doctor's suggestion.

● He knows there are some new treatments for the condition you have and wants expert advice on which is safest and most suitable for you.

● Your problem requires treatment he cannot provide, for instance surgery or biofeedback.

● If you have an uncommon disorder your GP will want guidance from a colleague who is fully conversant with it.

● He may find your symptoms puzzling and need expert help in tracking down the exact cause.

● The trouble does not seem to be responding to the standard treatment.

- Finally, you may have emotional, family or sexual problems you would rather not discuss with a doctor who also sees your partner or other family members.

STATE SYSTEM OR PRIVATELY-FUNDED MEDICAL CARE?

Either way you'll see an expert. Under the State system you cannot specify a particular doctor and you may have to wait longer for an appointment, but the advantages are that it doesn't cost you, plus the convenience of the back-up of all the hospital facilities on the spot. With a private appointment you have more choice about the timing, a more relaxed atmosphere, and no pressure from a crowded waiting room. It is worth checking whether either you or your partner is covered by a company group insurance scheme. A sensible compromise, if you are paying yourself, is to have one private consultation and State care to follow on.

The appointment: Usually your GP will write, explaining your case, and asking for an appointment to be sent to you. If it is urgent he will also telephone. If it is not especially urgent, but you have not heard within ten days, or you feel worse, telephone your GP and the hospital, or the private consultant's secretary.

Preparing for the appointment: As soon as you get the booking, switch off your worry. You have taken positive action towards sorting out your problem and it's over to the experts now.

- Reckon on a whole morning or afternoon being used up.
- Fix for a friend to go with you. You can feel a little lost after a medical consultation, and a cup of tea with someone familiar puts it in perspective.
- Choose clothes that are easy to take on and off. In

particular avoid long, tight sleeves, which make it awkward to take your blood pressure, or lace-up footwear which takes an age to undo before you can even be weighed. Even if you are to see a psychiatrist or a throat specialist, be prepared for a physical.

- Mention first the symptom or problem that bothers you most *now*. When and how did it start? Have you or any relative had anything similar before?
- Expect to be asked about alcohol, tobacco and your lifestyle.
- Remind yourself of key dates in your life: birth, marriage, children, bereavements.
- Medicines: make an exact list, or take the actual containers.

TYPES OF SPECIALIST

Dermatologist: Skin specialist. Don't feel cheated if he only sees you for five minutes after you've been waiting weeks for the appointment. He will have the expertise to recognize 90% of skin diseases on sight.

Gynaecologist: For 'women's problems'. It is difficult not to feel embarrassed, but the doctor's only concern is to find out what is wrong, so that he or she can put it right. An internal examination is no more to him than looking in your mouth to a dentist.

Surgeon: Operative treatment is the quickest of all, and anaesthetics and pain-killers will save you from most of the pain.

The types of surgeon include cosmetic (for making you look better), orthopaedic (for bones and joints), genito-urinary (for bladder and reproductive organs), neurosurgeons (for nerves: not the emotional type).

Physician: A doctor who deals with physical illness but does not operate. There are general physicians, but most have a specialty: cardiologists for the heart and blood vessels; rheumatologists for joints and muscles; nephrologists for the kidneys; oncologists for cancers; endocrinologists for glands; and radiologists: experts in X-rays and similar techniques.

Psychiatrists: Doctors who deal with emotional problems and illnesses that affect feeling and thinking. Don't feel insulted if your doctor suggests that you should see a psychiatrist. You are in company with many sensitive, distinguished people. Depression or anxiety, for example, cause more suffering and more upset to a person's life than a broken leg or pneumonia.

Clinical psychologists: are not doctors but are skilled in testing mental function and in giving some forms of talking treatment. Psychotherapists may be doctors, psychologists, or anyone who has done a course in helping people through talking. Counsellors are often nurses: they have done a course in rather practical talking.

Investigations

Sometimes when you consult your family doctor, and almost invariably when you see a specialist, he or she will arrange several tests to find out more about how your body is functioning.

Urine tests and urinalysis give information on disorders or infections of the water system and some general problems, like diabetes.

Blood tests are the most useful of all, throwing light on the working of almost every part of your body, from the blood itself to your liver, thyroid or immunity system.

X-rays provide see-through pictures of your bones and

other organs. Special types of X-ray include barium meals and barium enemas for the digestive tract, pyelograms for the kidneys and chest X-rays for the lungs.

CAT (computerized axial tomography) scans give multiple pictures as though the part scanned had been cut into slices.

PET (positron emission tomography) scans show in picture form the metabolism in different areas.

MRI (magnetic resonance imaging) also gives more detailed information than ordinary X-ray.

Ultrasound gives a moving photograph of some internal parts and is used in investigating the abdomen, or the heart when it is called *echocardiography*.

ECG (electrocardiogram) or EKG makes a record of the electrical activity in the heart, which reflects how well it is working.

EEG (electroencephalogram) does the same thing for the brain.

Most investigations are not even uncomfortable, and they often obviate the need for look-see surgery, such as laparoscopy, or endoscopy: the passing of a thin fibre-optic tube into the stomach, chest or back passage.

Treatment

Once he has a working idea of what the problem is, your doctor can decide on treatment. The main categories are:

Prophylactic: To prevent your developing some disorder to which you are susceptible, perhaps more than other people. Babies and travellers have various inoculations or tablets to protect them from infection with, say, measles or malaria. If your chest is your weak spot, you may decide to have an anti-flu jab before the winter, or if there's breast cancer in your family your doctor may suggest an anti-oestrogen.

All other types of treatment aim to make you feel better.

Palliatives: These don't deal directly with the cause, but control the symptoms. Examples are aspirin for a headache, whatever brought it on, or a soothing linctus for a cough.

Curative treatment: This aims to get at the root of the trouble. This is usually *physical*; that includes medication, surgery, physiotherapy and various forms of ray: infra-red, ultraviolet and radiotherapy.

Medication

This is the most used and most important form of treatment, and usually the most convenient, since you can carry it around with you.

Side-effects: These are the unwanted effects you may get from drugs as well as those the doctor is aiming for. In most cases you will not experience any side-effects at all, but if you do they are likely to arise when you first take the drug and your body is adjusting to it. A few drugs only produce side-effects when you have been taking them for some time. Antibiotics tend to cause loose motions after about two weeks, and major tranquillizers can lead to a tremor after several months or years.

Most side-effects are harmless, if uncomfortable. Dry mouth is common with antidepressants, and daytime drowsiness from 'sleepers' the night before, or anti-histamines for allergic reactions. Indigestion can be caused by various tablets taken on an empty stomach:

aspirin, steroids, non-steroid medicines for arthritis. Beta-blockers, of which the commonest is Inderal, are used to slow the heart and lower the blood pressure. They can also make you feel tired and have cold hands and feet.

If you develop some unpleasant symptom which you suspect may be connected with medicine you've started recently, check with your doctor. If you are having side-effects he or she will advise you whether to stop the drug, reduce the dose, or soldier on. Peculiar sensations or symptoms are unlikely to be side-effects.

Habit-forming: Next to side-effects, what people most fear is getting hooked on a medicine. Fortunately, most medicines are not addictive, and this goes for anti-depressants, antibiotics, blood pressure drugs and those for diabetes, among many. The best known chemical group which can cause trouble – for susceptible people – are the benzodiazepines. These are the anti-anxiety or minor tranquillizers, and the 'sleepers' or hypnotics. Common examples are diazepam (Valium), lorazepam (Ativan), and nitrazepam (Mogadon).

Other types of medicine which are difficult to give up include some steroids, such as prednisolone, slimming tablets such as diethylpropion (Tenuate Dospan), pain-killers such as co-praxamol or Diagesic, and of course many of the illegally obtained social drugs.

There is no drug, however long you've been taking it, that you cannot get off, with your doctor's help if necessary. It is important not to try to give up medicines, for instance to control your blood pressure, which are needed to keep you well.

Special points for over-sixties

Medicines are just as useful to you now as before, but your body may deal with them slightly differently.

Most people in their 60s and beyond find that they get as much effect from a slightly smaller amount of whisky or wine than previously. This is because the liver works at a more relaxed pace. Similarly, the many drugs which are metabolized in the liver before they can be discarded now tend to build up in your body – even at the same dosage. Elimination via the kidney/urine system is also slower, and added to this there is less so-called binding of drugs to protein in the blood. The result is that for the same dose of medicine, the concentration in your blood increases to four times as much over the years 40 to 70.

This means that you need smaller amounts for the same effect. Otherwise you may get into a near-overdose situation. Long-acting diabetic drugs (not insulin) can be definitely dangerous at what had been your normal dose. Chlorpropamide is one that should probably be avoided, now. Other medicines to check with your doctor, particularly if you have been taking them for a long time, include pain-killers, anti-arthritis drugs, tetracycline, antidepressants, sleeping tablets, digoxin, anti-anxiety tablets, beta-blockers, penicillin and warfarin. Side-effects are likelier, of course, with a high level of the drug in your blood. Besides, your system tends to be more sensitive nowadays.

Absorption of medicines: Although 80% of medicines are absorbed just as completely at 80 as at 20, the process becomes gradually slower from about 25. By the time you are 60 this will be noticeable. You may find you take a little longer to feel merry after an alcoholic drink, or more obviously that the aspirin is slightly slower in relieving your headache. If you are on a diuretic, a tablet to stimulate you to pass water, you may find it better, now, to delay taking it until you are back home from any outing planned, rather than in the morning. It may not have worked before you go. Among other substances absorbed more slowly are glucose, and vitamins C and Bl (thiamine).

Antacid medicines, used for indigestion, definitely delay the effects of aspirin, paracetamol, tetracycline, major tranquillizers like thioridazine, and levodopa (Sinemet) used in Parkinson's disease.

Over-the-counter medicines: However herbal, green and organic, these too can have side-effects, and some are habit-forming. The latter include some pain-killers, cold cures and anti-diarrhoea medicine. Side-effects from the type of cold cure that aims to dry up a runny nose include difficulty in passing water and even mental confusion – if you are susceptible.

Commonly-used medicines

Of course you will ask your doctor what you want to know about any drugs he prescribes, but it may be useful to run through the basics.

DRUGS FOR THE DIGESTIVE SYSTEM

Antacids: These are used for indigestion. The type based on aluminium salts tend to be constipating (e.g. Gelusil, Aludrox), while those based on magnesium have a mild laxative effect. Some have both constituents, e.g. Gaviscon. They are best taken between meals and at night, preferably not with other medicines.

Ulcer-healing medicines: They are magically effective, and side-effects are almost unknown. The longest-established are cimetidine (Tagamet) and ranitidine (Zantac).

Antidiarrhoeals: Taking plenty of fluid is more important than any medicines, some of which have side-effects or are habit-forming if they contain codeine or morphine.

Laxatives: They come in two kinds.

Bulk-producers are the safest: from ispaghula husk (Fybogel, Metamucil) or bran (Fybranta). You need to take extra fluid with these, and they can cause bloating and flatulence. Bran can interfere with your absorbing iron and calcium: the blood and bone minerals.

Stimulants: These include senna, cascara, danthron and the chocolate laxatives. They should not be used regularly: in the short term they cause stomach cramps and over a longer period wear out the colon, so that it becomes too slack to function.

WATER TABLETS (DIURETICS)

These are given to help you to get rid of excess fluid, by passing water. They are particularly valuable in heart, blood pressure and liver problems, but not so useful in the common type of ankle swelling, due to gravity not disease. There is a wide choice of diuretics, but they are a strain on the kidneys, and may interfere with such minerals as potassium in your blood. Unless they are really necessary it is better not to continue taking them indefinitely. They cause stomach pain in some people.

BETA-BLOCKERS

These drugs slow the heart and lower the blood pressure, and are often given along with a diuretic. In small doses they are sometimes prescribed for anxiety. You should not take these if you have asthma or another airways disorder. Common side-effects are fatigue, cold hands and feet, and less often, digestive disturbance.

HEART DRUGS

Angina Tablets – glyceryl trinitrate (nitroglycerin) – dissolved under the tongue is the usual treatment for angina. It is effective for about half-an-hour, or longer with the slow-release form. Possible side-effects are headache and flushing.

Warfarin: This reduces the risk of coronary thrombosis, clot-formation in an artery supplying the heart. The dose must be just right, to avoid unwanted bleeding. Aspirin is a gentler anticoagulant.

Digoxin: The standard heart strengthening and regulating medicine. It can upset the appetite or cause fatigue.

MEDICINES TO HELP WITH BREATHING

Salbutamol (Ventolin): Taken from an inhaler, this is the best-known of the medicines which open up the airways. It seldom causes side-effects.

Beclomethasone (Becotide): A steroid which doesn't get into the general system, taken by inhaler. It is useful for persistent asthma.

Cromoglycate (Intal): Inhaled as a powder, this is useful in preventing asthma attacks, not treating them.

Antihistamines: These anti-allergy drugs are used in hay fever, itchy allergic rashes, insect bites and drug allergies. They all make you feel drowsy, dangerous for driving, and may give you a dry mouth. They include Phenergan (promethiazine), chlorpheniramine, and the least sedating, terfenadine.

COUGH MEDICINES

These are rather unsatisfactory. Most of those meant to settle a tickly cough are based on codeine or a related compound. They are constipating, habit-forming if you take them for long, and can be harmful if you have bronchitis or emphysema. Simple linctus – or honey and lemon – is soothing and at least does no harm. Medicines that are meant to loosen a tight cough – don't.

Decongestants, to clear the nose: The type you inhale have a rebound effect: your nose runs even more copiously when the effect wears off. The type you swallow, including over-the-counter cold cures don't lead to rebound, but can cause a rise in blood pressure, headache and palpitations if you take too much or are sensitive.

SLEEPING MEDICINES AND DAYTIME SEDATIVES

Nearly all of these are from the benzodiazepine family, and they include the best and the safest of such drugs. They are useful in a brief emergency, for a period no longer than a fortnight. As mentioned above, they are habit-forming in some people over time, and withdrawal effects may occur if they are suddenly stopped. They interfere with learning and memory, and those taken at night often lead to a hangover effect and inefficiency the following day.

Hypnotics ('sleepers') include long-acting flurazepam and nitrazepam (Dalmane and Mogadon) and short-acting temazepam. Other chemicals such as zopiclone, chloral and chlormethiazole have no advantages over the benzodiazepines.

ANTIDEPRESSANTS

These have a wonderful effect on certain types of depressive illness, as opposed to passing unhappiness or ingrained dissatisfaction. Unfortunately it is usually about ten days after the medication is started before the depression lifts. Side-effects, if they occur, tend to come on early and improve after four or five days. They include dry mouth, drowsiness, constipation and difficulty in focusing to read. Amitriptyline and imipramine are the longest established, but more recent formulations include Ludiomil, trazodone and mianserin – with fewer side-effects.

More recently a new group has been developed: fluoxetine, fluvoxamine and sertraline. These may cause a drop in appetite, even discomfort, and less sound sleep. They are used in bulimia, bouts of over-eating, as well as depression. They are best taken after food.

PAIN-KILLERS (ANALGESICS)

Aspirin and paracetamol (acetaminophen) are invaluable for mild to moderate pain and also fever. Some people are sensitive to aspirin; others find it irritates their stomach. This is reduced by taking the tablets with or after food. Side-effects are less likely with paracetamol (acetaminophen). Ibuprofen is especially useful in pain due to arthritic or rheumatic aches and pains.

A number of pain-killers comprise more than one drug, for instance Equagesic, Distalgesic, Veganin and Synalgos. The stronger analgesics are only available through a doctor: they have mental side-effects, as we know by heroin addiction. People with severe pain don't become addicted, so this is no problem if you ever need such drugs.

ANTIBIOTICS

These help you to fight off infections.

The penicillins include amoxycillin (amoxicillin) and flucloxacillin. Most of them are given in six-hourly doses, day and night. People with a special sensitivity may develop a rash and fever. Such an allergic reaction means that you cannot use any of the penicillins. Most people develop loose motions after more than ten days on an antibiotic. This is not an allergic reaction, but due to a temporary upset of the normal bacteria in the intestines.

To get the best result from antibiotics they should be taken when the stomach has no food in it, but not too soon before a meal.

Erythromycin and tetracycline are alternatives, useful for those allergic to penicillin. Abdominal discomfort may be caused by large doses of either drug.

Nitrofurantoin (Furadantin) is an antibiotic which is particularly useful in urinary infections. While it suits most people, in some there may be side-effects including nausea. It is best taken with food.

MEDICINES FOR JOINT AND MUSCLE PROBLEMS

The keystone of treatment are NSAIDs (non-steroidal anti-inflammatory drugs), reducing both pain and inflammation. Unfortunately they are unsuitable for anyone who has had a stomach or duodenal ulcer, and tend to make some asthmatics worse. We over-60s are more likely to get side-effects such as digestive discomfort, diarrhoea, rash or headache. The trick is to start with a low dose and work up to what is effective – and not to stay on the medicine when our symptoms have subsided.

For those who cannot tolerate the tablets, there are preparations to rub in over the painful area: for instance piroxicam (Feldene) gel. The NSAID type of cream or gel is more effective than old-fashioned creams and balsams – but there is a small risk for asthmatics (but not for stomach upset).

Nurofen (ibuprofen) is an NSAID you can buy without prescription; those you can get through your doctor include Naprosyn, and the longer-acting piroxicam

(Feldene) which you need take only once a day.

Aspirin is useful for joint and rheumatic pain instead of an NSAID. Paracetamol (acetaminophen) is kinder to the stomach, but not quite as effective.

SKIN PREPARATIONS

Creams mix in with the skin's own moisture, so they are easy to apply and soak in. Barrier creams are mildly waterproof and protect the skin from irritation by urine or other fluids.

Ointments are greasy and suitable for very dry areas.

Lotions and sprays are fluid and can be either watery or slightly oily.

All these preparations can be used to apply various medicines, but often the simplest, drug-free applications are the best.

Itching: Calamine cream or lotion is as good as anything and causes no adverse effects. Antihistamine creams and local anaesthetics can produce a reaction in the skin, but antihistamine tablets don't have this disadvantage.

Steroid creams and ointments work remarkably effectively on inflamed skin, but there are snags and sometimes side-effects. A rebound worsening of the condition often arises when you try to stop using the application, but if you use it for more than three or four weeks you may develop long-term thinning of the skin in the affected area, with loss of colour and a growth of downy hair. There is also a risk of causing general physical upset if a potent steroid is used on a wide area of skin.

The steroid skin preparations are categorized by potency from 1 to 4. The mildest, hydrocortisone cream rates potency 1; the most potent, rating 4, are flurandrenolone and clobetasol.

Taking medicines and stopping them

No-one is perfect and it is easy to forget the odd dose of medicine. Often this does not matter much, but with antibiotics, for example, it is important to keep the level of the medicine steady in the blood. It is also important with these drugs to complete the course, however much better you feel. Half-finished courses enable bacteria to develop resistance to antibiotics, while in illnesses like depression it makes relapse more likely. If you have side-effects, or think you may, call your doctor for advice. Don't suffer in silence and don't throw the tablets away.

Withdrawal effects: The concept may worry you – unnecessarily. In fact, only the 'sleepers' and day-time 'calmers' (minor tranquillizers) produce withdrawal symptoms, and then only if you stop them too suddenly. The effects are sleeplessness and sharp anxiety, with all that entails. The answer is to come off more slowly.

Psychotherapy

Medication is one major form of treatment. The talking treatments are another. There are several types:

SUPPORTIVE PSYCHOTHERAPY AND COUNSELLING

These comprise reassuring and helpful discussion, often including practical suggestions. You may get this on an individual basis or in a group, led by a therapist.

SELF-HELP GROUPS

These are increasingly popular, and are run entirely by the people who share a similar problem. It may be an eating disorder, a serious physical illness, or a psychological problem.

Psychoanalysis: The traditional lying on a couch scene – shades of Freud. It lasts a couple of years with five sessions a week, which costs. It helps you to understand yourself by re-running and re-feeling the events in your life from Day One. Usually it is those who have not long achieved adult status who go in for this.

Brief psychotherapy: This operates on analytical theories but is more down-to-earth and lasts for up to six months.

Cognitive therapy: This is a treatment for mild anxiety and depressive states. It comprises a training in altering negative attitudes and responses in the here and now. Usually there are ten sessions at weekly intervals.

Behaviour therapy: This is even more down-to-earth. It is a method of overcoming either compulsions to do something repeatedly, or phobias. These are unreasonable fears of, for instance, travelling. You are helped and coerced into a different pattern of behaviour. It is like breaking a spell. This is short and effective treatment and increases general confidence.

Hypnotherapy: Anyone can be hypnotized if they want to be, but no-one can be induced by hypnosis to do something against their principles, or that they really don't want. It is useful for helping people who genuinely want to kick a bad habit like smoking, or to overcome a fear of failure, such as writer's block.

The psychotherapies can be given by any one of these: a doctor who is also a psychiatrist, a psychoanalyst who may or may not be a doctor, a psychologist, and also a family doctor, or a nurse or social worker who has some relevant training. The last three usually provide counselling: sensible, informed discussion of problems in a supportive atmosphere. There are also lay therapists who have no link with medicine, but have had psychotherapy training: there are various types from neurolinguistic programming to scream therapy.

Complementary or alternative medicine

Straight scientific medicine has made phenomenal strides in the last century-and-a-half, but its focus on diseases and their treatment tends to bypass the individual patient who is suffering. It is dehumanizing to be categorized a diabetic, a schizophrenic or worse still – a geriatric. I am Joan Gomez.

The complementary therapies are an extraordinarily diverse assortment, from acupuncture, hallowed by 4000 years of practice, to the Alexander technique, introduced in our century. But they all put you, the person needing help, at the centre. They hold that health means more than an absence of symptoms, and recovery includes harmonization with your surroundings. Diagnosis isn't merely the name of a disease, say shingles, but is expressed in terms of imbalance, malfunction or misplacement. Instead of scientific investigations to find out what is wrong, such as blood tests, X-rays or electrocardiograms, complementary therapists rely on sensitive observation of, for instance, the sheen on the skin, the timbre of the voice or the texture of the pulse. The Chinese search for signs in the outer ear of distant disorders, while osteopaths assess the emotional state from the tension in various parts of the body. In psychic diagnosis the therapist visualizes an aura round the patient or areas of light and shade on his body.

In complementary medicine there is an emphasis on

utilizing the self-healing powers of the mind-body unit (if you cut your finger you see this in action). In all the therapies you receive more or less instruction on how to revamp your lifestyle to achieve greater contentment. There is satisfaction in feeling that you are helping yourself.

Complementary methods are particularly valuable for alleviating long-term and wear-and-tear health problems and the psychosomatic group. They are not so useful in acute illnesses like influenza or for injuries, and can be dangerous if used on their own in serious disorders like cancer. Nor should you expect a one-off consultation and cure. Because you will have new concepts to learn and changes in your life, you will need a course of treatment.

HOLISTIC MEDICINE

This is especially helpful in stress-related and chronic disorders that don't clear up. The aim is the 'optimal attunement of body, mind, emotion and spirit'. It comfortably augments conventional treatments. Holistic practitioners, rather like psychiatrists, want to know every last detail of your life, from birth or before, and what your symptoms mean to you. The treatment is talk.

THE ALEXANDER TECHNIQUE

F. M. Alexander was a Shakespearean actor who found that he moved awkwardly on stage, ruining his whole performance. He worked out a better way of managing his body, and benefited so much that he taught the method to others. His technique of re-education of your posture, movements and bearing lead to a feeling of effortless freedom – of mind and body.

EURYTHMY

Like the Alexander technique, it trains you in movement, and also in speech, as an art. It was developed by Rudolf Steiner, an educationist.

CHIROPRACTIC

This began around 1895 on the principle that most of what goes wrong with the joints and bones is due to inaccurate alignment of the vertebrae: the small bones which make up the spine. This bad fit is thought to press on the nerves and thereby cause problems in the rest of the body.

OSTEOPATHY

This system was developed by Andew Still in Missouri about the same time as chiropractic. The underlying idea about the spine is similar, except that Still believed that it was the circulation of the blood, rather than the nerves, that was impaired by misplaced vertebrae. Under both theories the treatment is manipulation, and it is often particularly successful for a stiff, painful neck, shoulder or back. People often feel better all round after the massage and manipulation.

NATUROPATHY

It defines itself as 'a system of treating human ailments which recognizes that healing depends upon the vital curative force within the human organism'. Most of us, including doctors would agree. Naturopathy began with a middle European farmer and a weaver who found they suffered less from rheumatism on a certain strict diet.

A number of naturopathic therapists use iridology: the diagnosis of disorders through examination of the coloured iris of the eye. The idea arose when a Prussian priest accidentally broke the leg of his pet owl, and noticed a change in the bird's eyes. Naturopaths are concerned to assess your vital strengths and reserves, rather than concentrating on your faults and weaknesses. Their diagnosis sounds different from the medical style. For example, 'eczema' or 'psoriasis' might be replaced by 'underactivity of the skin'.

Naturopathic treatment usually focuses on diet, although in some clinics they take the opposite corner and concentrate on elimination and purification. The recommended diet in general is based on organically-grown, additive-free, wholefoods with a high fibre content. Not everyone can cope with this, depending on their digestive system. Days of fasting or fruit only are often advised.

NUTRITION THERAPY

This is allied to naturopathy, and like anything that encourages us to eat, is popular in the US. The idea is that we may be short of essential nutrients without realizing it. Vitamins and minerals are added to the diet, and allergies sought by exclusion dieting: basically seeing if you feel better or worse without certain classes of foods, say dairy products. There are dangers in overdoing the vitamin intake, particularly A and D which can be toxic, E which can put your blood pressure up, or nicotinic acid from the B group which can lower it too far, and even C which can raise your cholesterol level and in some people cause nausea. It's safest to take your vitamins in foods, and more enjoyable.

HOMOEOPATHY

Homoeopathy was put on the map as a system of healing by a Dr Hahnemann around 1811. The key element is the use of tiny amounts of herbs or drugs to stimulate the body's defences, an idea from ancient Greece. Hahnemann was concerned with physical illness, but a hundred years later Dr Edward Bach made dilute essences from flowers and twigs which he used to correct the emotional disarray which may underlie disease.

HERBALISM

The use of herbal remedies is part of homoeopathy, naturopathy and traditional Chinese medicine. It is used to cure rather than prevent illness. Digitalis from foxgloves and aspirin from the willow are examples of the powerful medicines in plants. Camomile has long been known as a calmative, rosemary is said to relieve pain, and mint to pep up the circulation. Except in homoeopathy, in which only minute quantities are used, herbal medicines can have side-effects like the rest.

Ginseng can raise your blood pressure, cause sore breasts, ankle swelling or headache, and it is mildly addictive. Some of the herbal teas naturally contain cocaine, while synthetic steroids are sometimes added illegally to so-called herbal preparations. Licorice can upset your metabolism and make your muscles weak. The sensible approach is not to get too enthusiastic in taking any medicines, and stop if you have doubts. Serious research is urgently needed.

AROMATHERAPY

This employs essential oils from plants, to use as an adjunct to massage. Different essences are used to produce different effects, for instance basil to lift the mood. The whole process is deliciously relaxing.

TRADITIONAL CHINESE MEDICINE

The idea is to keep you well. Patients have regular seasonal examinations – and pay the doctor when there is nothing wrong! The main components of the system are acupuncture, herbs and exercises. The well-being of the mind-body unit depends on the balance between your yin (the North side of a mountain) and your yang, your sunny side. It also requires chi, the vital life force, flowing from the environment through your body. T'ai-chi are exercises done by many Chinese every morning to get the chi flowing nicely. Better than jogging.

ACUPUNCTURE

This has been practised in the East for thousands of years, but was only used in England from about 1820. Ten to fifteen needles are inserted and twisted over what is judged to be the trigger area for a particular pain or unpleasant emotion. Three thousand years ago Ling Shu wrote: 'In pain, puncture the tender point.' Today acupuncture is widely available, including in the National Health Service, and there is no doubt that it is effective for some people. You need to have three or four sessions to judge whether it will work for you. The needles are extremely fine and hardly hurt, but you need a well-trained operator to avoid the risk of bleeding, or of accidentally introducing infection. About 50% of patients feel drowsy after the treatment – probably from the release of endorphins, the body's self-made analgesics.

TENS

Transcutaneous electrical nerve stimulation is a development from the 1970s of acupuncture with needles. Instead, electrodes are placed over the acupuncture points and a current passed. It is not quite as effective as acupuncture but more convenient. You can hire the apparatus for use at home, if you are suffering from chronic pain. There are no side-effects, but you mustn't use TENS if you have a pace-maker.

REFLEXOLOGY

This has also come to us from Chinese medicine, and comprises both diagnosis and treatment. The idea is that on the soles of the feet is a map of the body parts, and a form of massage to the foot relieves problems in the different areas. Like aromatherapy, reflexology can make you feel peaceful and pleasant.

Complementary therapies won't save your life, but they can sometimes make it more worth living. If you have aches and pains that won't go away, are constantly under stress or your mind-body unit isn't functioning smoothly, and your doctor has run out of ideas, this is the time to turn to the alternatives. If you or your partner have the misfortune to develop a serious medical condition you need all the help you can get. Take all that straightforward medicine can offer, and top it up with complementary therapy, hedging your bets.

Chapter 6

Sex, love and romance

'Love does not consist in gazing at each other but at looking outward together in the same direction.'

Antoine de Saint Exupery

Sex, love, romance: all these fundamental aspects of being a human being give our lives warmth and meaning – at every age. The emphasis changes with maturity, from wham-bang bonking (ranking top in teenage) to a deeper, richer sense of loving during adulthood. This enlarges to include mind as well as body. It gains an element of responsibility and encompasses our children – and others. Always the silver thread of sex runs through, lighting everything: the special love between a man and a woman for most of us, and man to man or woman to woman for the minority.

The emotional developments at 60-plus are all positive, but the physical modifications need to be understood. Like all our hormones, the self-made chemicals which influence both our feelings and how our bodies function, the sex hormones run to a rhythm. Women learn very well the monthly rhythm with its characteristic shifts in mood, punctuated by the periods. For men as well as women there are rhythms which operate over weeks, over the seasons or the years. We all know where a young man's fancy turns in spring – and there is a broad sweep of changes over a lifetime.

The menopause affects both sexes, but the female more dramatically. In evolutionary terms it is a recent human innovation. It allows for the continuance of sexual enjoyment without the complication of pregnancy at an inconvenient phase of life. When the ovaries stop releasing a monthly ovum (egg) the manufacture of the female hormone, oestrogen, is taken over by the adrenal glands. By 60 this arrangement will be working smoothly and the symptoms of the change-over, such as hot flushes, will be irritations of the past.

Hormone Replacement Therapy (HRT), basically oestrogen, can be helpful to many women, especially during the first few years after the change. It may be continued indefinitely if you have neither fibroids, high blood pressure, some breast problems nor a clotting tendency. HRT is good for the bones, joints and skin, but does not actually boost your sexual interest.

The male menopause comes a few years later and is more gradual, but there is the same emotional turmoil, expressed differently. Men often suffer more anxiety. A woman of 60, 70 or 80 can easily indulge in intercourse, with the help of a lubricant if necessary. For a man of 60 it can be alarming that his erections take longer to come, are less rock-hard and don't last so long. There are fewer spontaneous morning erections, too. Everything physical about this phase of life is gentler and a little slower. This is nothing to do with quality. A Daimler may not be the fastest, but what a gorgeous ride!

Because of the worry about failure some men in the prime of life try for younger partners, or resort to call-girls or to rent-boys in a way they would not have dreamed of earlier. This is reflected in the unexpectedly large number of cases of HIV infection and other sexually-transmitted diseases (STD) among men of this age. Occasionally the normal, harmless enlargement of the prostate gland induces strong sexual urges, which may lead a man into out-of-character behaviour. Having reached a 'sensible age', and perhaps high office, confers no immunity to sexual infection. And we have all heard horror stories of bishops, lawyers, politicians and doctors who have done something sexually reckless in middle age.

In general, for both sexes in maturity, the flow of blood to the sexual areas is less easily stimulated and less intense. For men this means the erectile changes already described, for women a reduced secretion of vaginal fluid. In a few, less than one in ten, this relative dryness leads to soreness (vaginitis) requiring an oestrogen cream. But nearly half 60-year-old women find intercourse more comfortable with a simple lubricant such as KY jelly or the new intimate moisturizer, Replens.

A handful of medical problems can interfere with sexual function, especially for men: diabetes, heart disorders, arthritis, embarrassing stress incontinence, and some medicines. These include the thiazide class of water tablet, beta-blockers for high blood pressure, anti-depressants, 'sleepers' and tranquillizers; but alcohol is worse than any of these. However, genuinely poor health is not nearly as likely to preclude sexual intercourse as the belief that you aren't competent, or a lack of interest.

The trend

There is an undoubted tendency, more clear-cut in men whatever they say, for a reduction in sexual activity from age 50. Intimacy becomes more marital, a sharing of all aspects of life, rather than just sex. There is the most enormous variation between individuals, but these are the averages for couples in the decade 60 to 70:

1. 75% say they have intercourse once a week or more.
2. 50% say they do it in more than one position, and at different times of day.

3. 50% masturbate (and 23% at age 90 to 95).
4. 90% enjoy kissing, cuddling and bodily nearness – indefinitely:

> *Cedric*, 78, was a case in point. He had a serious illness, but even in the critical stage he asked his wife to lie on the bed next to him, whenever she visited the hospital. The Ward Sister was shocked, but Cedric and Alice didn't care.

5. Although they always enjoy physical affection, most men and women find that from around 68 they do not have the urgent impetus for intercourse that preoccupied them in youth. It's a matter of changing values.

The psychological reasons for a lessening of all-out sexual activity weigh much more than any physical limitations. Do any of these apply to you:

1. You may never have had a particularly rampant sexual drive – so why expect it now?
2. Monotony – with the same partner for so long. It can become as exciting as cleaning your teeth – unless you spice it up with extra care.
3. You may have developed more interest in food and drink over recent years – so that your sexual appetite is less important.
4. You now have other, more pressing preoccupations, and perhaps one of you is genuinely tired.
5. You feel unattractive, because of your figure or some other 'imperfection'. But is your partner as good as new?
6. You may be suffering from depression: nothing seems worthwhile. You need help.
7. Embarrassment: your children and their generation don't like to think of your having a sexual relationship. Have you noticed how the junk-mail advertisers

target you for thermal underwear nowadays instead of sex aids?

8. Some of us still have a hangover from the prudish attitudes and inadequate info provided by our own parents.
9. Fear of failure, especially for men who feel they should be an everlasting stud: one reason why masturbation is affected less over time than a partnership effort.
10. Loyalty among the widowed towards their former partners. Sad.
11. Lack of opportunities.

If full intercourse means a lot to you, remember that it works best, at any age, in the context of a loving relationship. Do you need to do anything on that score? Otherwise, rev up the fresh air and exercise, cut down on alcohol and consider rescheduling to the mornings for a frolic. Erections are at their best then, no-one is tired. What a splendid start to a day. There are, today, medical manoeuvres to help with erection problems, and the other difficulties that also affect younger men and women: premature ejaculation, spasm of the vagina (vaginismus), missing or mis-timed orgasm.

Although you haven't necessarily grown out of earlier sexual hang-ups, your great advantage is that you have already had experience of the simple physical act and now you can concentrate on exploring the subtler aspects of sex and sensuality.

Hormonal changes

After the change, women produce less oestrogen, the main female sex hormone, but also less male hormone – necessary for libido, or desire. For men there is a reduction in testosterone, the basic male hormone, and also alterations in three associated hormones. It is a complex modification in the hormonal mix that alters attitudes and feelings at this interesting age. HRT for women comprises mainly oestrogen: beneficial in several ways, but it does not directly increase libido. The still controversial HRT for men needs further development and modification to make it safe enough for general recommendation.

It is usually more rewarding to work with Nature than to attempt to turn the clock back chemically. Build up and enjoy closeness, understanding and tenderness. Find out anew what gives your partner most bodily delight – and what gives you the most pleasure: now. It would be very odd if your physical sensitivity and responsiveness had remained exactly the same as when you were a callow 20-year-old.

An essential is to allow time for sex. Just as you must keep your mind and body in training if they are to function at their best, so you must nourish your sensual nature with practice. The watchwords throughout are: USE IT OR LOSE IT. If you find you are often too busy or too tired, or can't be bothered to allocate a slot for sex: re-schedule. Kick off by reassuring your partner of his/her attractiveness, and don't expect all sexual activity to work perfectly. Think in terms of fun, not failure. A recent BBC series: 'Will you still love me?' about sex in the over-60s was up-beat, positive – and extremely popular. The range of people who took part, most of them much older than you, and their confident outlook were the antidote to anyone's sexual self-doubt.

Masturbation

Masturbation is an ugly-sounding word, and fragments of Victorian prudery still cling to it. It is a natural, super-safe and almost universal method of calming sexual tensions, and inducing bodily relaxation. If widowhood or some other reason leaves you without an available partner, it is a sensible way of keeping an essential part of you viable. It also provides a degree of comfort. If this has to be a major sexual outlet for you, make it dignified and important as well as private. Make the room comfortably warm, with soft music if you like that, and the telephone unplugged.

Partners

A serviceable marriage or partnership, with a sense of sharing and striving for the mutual good, is worth fostering. In purely practical terms, married men live longer and are healthier than those on their own or with a homosexual partner. Married women don't live any longer but they are generally happier than the others. Like any other complicated working machinery, marriage needs oiling, servicing and occasional repairs. This is a stage when much of the relationship has been taken for granted for years. Romance has been allowed to lapse. It is urgent to do a resuscitation job – using judicious praise, small presents and suggesting things the other would like to do. Hopefully this will revive some of the feelings you both used to have. At the very worst, if you've drifted an unbridgeable distance apart, keep to the courtesy, consideration and lack of criticism you would show towards a stranger who was sharing your house.

You may feel that you and your partner have already cracked the riddle of living happily together, and have come up with the idea of exclusive closeness. This has dangers, too. The most long-lasting relationships are those in which the time spent together feels like a treat, not the bread-and-butter of life. Smothering with affection may come over as clinging, which in turn may come over as controlling and demanding. This is as ruinous to happiness as indifference, resentment or jealousy.

Seeing other people takes time and trouble, but it matters more now than in the years when you were in the maelstrom of work and family life. Your partner can appreciate you better, by having others, not nearly as nice or familiar, to compare you with. Other people are also an insurance against future loneliness, should either of you ever find yourselves on your own.

> *The Rafts* were a devoted couple. Their little house, Arcadia, and each other were all they needed for contentment, after Ron's early retirement. Their son had emigrated to Australia. Isobel Raft had just popped out to the post on the evening she was killed in a hit-and-run accident. Ron couldn't think of anyone he could 'phone. He and Isobel hadn't bothered to keep in touch with the people they used to know, nor considered it worthwhile to make any new contacts.

A tiresome fact of life is the disparity of numbers between the sexes. Women are usually younger than their partners, even in these days of allegedly equal opportunity. Divorce is common, and men usually remarry downwards afterwards, often choosing someone resembling their ex-wife when she was younger. Added to this, women live an average of six to eight years longer than men. All of which adds up to four times as many women as men at 60 – and the score is even more lop-sided later. Among the alternative groups, male homosexual relationships, where one partner is definitely senior, often founder at this age, but lesbian partnerships, with the couple of much the same age are the most stable of any.

While no man need fear running short of the company of the opposite sex, for women it's a very different story. Even if you choose an evening class in carpentry or car maintenance, you'll find the participants predominantly female. Most of us would find a Toy Boy too expensive – and anyway there's more to share with a proper adult man. Dating agencies flood their older male clients with a bewildering choice, but many of them won't accept a woman of 60 on their books at all: or worse, they just take the fee.

Whether you are a man or a woman, mixing with other people of both sexes is beneficial to health, humour and mental stimulus. 60-plus is an excellent time to keep alert for opportunities to be a good friend. By sod's law such opportunities come at the most inconvenient moments. Your neighbour will break a leg just when your son and his new wife are coming to stay; your friend urgently wants a lift when it's pitch-dark, raining and you'd put the car away. On the other hand, now is a fine time to develop old or take up new interests, the sort you can share with others.

We may not be engulfed in a grand romantic passion, nor luxuriate in the solid security of a thirty-year-old marriage, but we can all savour the little parcels of affection bestowed on us by children and ancient relatives, people we meet of all ages, all walks of life. They add up to a worthwhile sense of being surrounded by good feeling. We need them all, so let's make someone's day by telling them how good they look, how clever they are, how kind. With any luck we'll get the same good news back.

Chapter 7

Beauty and personality

'Laura was blooming still, had made the best
Of time, and time returned the compliment.'
Lord Byron

It is instantly recognizable – but who can say what beauty
is? And what about the charm, without which it is like
an unlit lamp? Youth, the obsession of our culture, is a
factor but by no means the whole scene. Sad that some
women, and men assessing women, seem to think it is.
It is better for men, because they are judged by women,
whose values are not as superficial as theirs. A man may
be considered more attractive with the passage of time if
his features denote strength, character and masculine
energy. A touch of grey at the temples is a positive bonus.

For the instant appraisal, what matters is what shows:
skin, teeth, hair, shape and clothes. The young don't have
a monopoly of these. We too have complexions, figures
and the rest. The difference is that we have to take a little
more thought and trouble. How lucky that we live in a
world where there is a wide choice of tactics to optimize
the way we look. Know-how is on tap, too.

The glow of good health, resulting from reasonable
amounts of food, sleep, exercise, fun and fresh air, forms
the basis: for either sex. It is reflected in your colour, clear
eyes, shining hair and supple body. If there is a medical

reason why you cannot be fully fit, it is all the more important to achieve the appealing charm of well-cared-for delicacy. Never think it doesn't matter. To look your best is a courtesy and a compliment to other people, and a necessary tonic to your own self-esteem.

Men are particularly prone to stop bothering when they are not actually in their work-place, and can develop an attachment to a disgusting old garment, like a toddler's comfort-toy.

Your skin

To recap from Chapter 2: your skin tends to become paler (unless you've cooked it) drier and more delicate than earlier. Male or female, your skin will lap up regular applications of a simple Vaseline-based lotion, better than lanolin, on the exposed parts, plus a sunscreen at the slightest sign of ultraviolet. This latter precaution delays the development of wrinkles and sags, but there is no total escape. Booze and tobacco speed the damage.

Among 30 beautiful women, age-range 20 to 80, the top tips for an ageless complexion are:

- The Cleopatra gimmick: washing at least your face in milk.
- The Meryl Streep method: never allow the sun to shine directly on your skin.
- Never drink spirits; stick to champagne.
- Use bath oils, never detergent-based bubble-baths.
- Allow the skin to absorb water by patting off the surplus, not drying thoroughly.
- To avoid the prune look, don't slim fast or to excess.
- Cultivate people who make you smile: it is the cross, anxious or glum expression lines that are unattractive.

Drastic measures

If you are in the media and your appearance is your livelihood, or you are desperately unhappy about bags, sags and wrinkles affecting your face, jack in your next holiday, including the time and the cost, and consult a top-class cosmetic surgeon. Have a look at someone else who has been through his hands.

- *Collagen implants* under the skin are made rapidly on a day-case basis, and cost around £150 in the UK (about $500 in USA and A$460 in Australia). The best age for this, say the surgeons, is around 45, but they will take on people up to 75. The effect lasts about six months. Madonna had the shape of her mouth adjusted by this method – they say.
- *Mini face-lift:* The operation takes about half-an-hour and involves some pain; you don't have to stay in overnight. The effect is not dramatic and may be disappointing, but it lasts about five years. Cost is around £500 in the UK (about $1200 in USA and A$1300–1900 in Australia).
- *Abrasion:* This means removal of the top two layers of the skin. The hope is that they will regrow fresh and new, without wrinkles. This again works best for those in the 40s and early 50s: the expression lines are too deep to erase later. The cost is £1000-plus in the UK ($2000–3000 in USA and A$2000 in Australia – if available) and you need to stay in the clinic a few nights.
- *Full face-lift:* It takes several weeks before you are fit to be seen, but is the most radical make-over. Again it does not last for much more than five years, and repeat operations give you the tambourine look – skin stretched thin and tight over the bones. Cost is about £5000 in the UK (about $9000–12,000 in USA and A$3000 in Australia). If it's cheaper, beware. You need

an artistically-sensitive, experienced surgeon if you are to come out of the process better rather than worse than before.

● *Dental make-over:* Plumb in the middle of your face is your smile – made or marred by your teeth. Have you any discoloured or chipped teeth which need capping, or dark metal fillings near the front that could be replaced by porcelain? If you have dentures that shift about when you laugh or bite an apple, discuss with your dental surgeon a new set, and pegging or other surgical procedures.

● *Liposuction:* This painful procedure has become increasingly popular as a surgical method of getting rid of fatty tissue. It can be very effective in the age range 20 to 50, but is not for our age group. Nor is the more recent operation of inserting a plastic 'girdle' in the abdomen. Our bodies respond best to the natural manoeuvres of diet and exercise.

Make-up

The most flattering foundation at this stage is moisturizing and in a light, warm shade to blend in with your skin colour but counteract the tendency to a greyish tinge. Follow on by brushing over loose translucent powder: your skin will look its best these days slightly veiled by the powder. Use eye, eyebrow and lip preparations in an understated way. Detailed, meticulous care pays off: bold, strong lines and colours are out. In particular choose a barely detectable lipstick, without gloss, but never imagine you can get away with omitting any face care.

Men have naturally more robust skins but many benefit from using a moisturizer. Shaving can damage your skin if it is starved dry. Nowadays that bronzed-by-the-great-outdoors look is out even for men, since we all know the dangers of sun damage. Of course, if you have a naturally brown skin it will be wonderfully resistant to wear-and-tear and age changes.

Hair

Above all, treat your hair kindly: no blow-drying, no vigorous brushing, no dragging a comb through it when it's wet, and avoid putting harsh chemicals on it as far as possible. If you must wave or colour it, choose the gentlest preparation available and test it on a strand that doesn't frame your face. Cream rinses and conditioners combat the dryness, but it makes no difference whether or not they are 'protein-enriched'. A silicone-based thickener gives the hair extra body.

If you are a woman, give your facial lines a lift with a short style, though not straight and flat, or else sweep it up high on your head. Anything near shoulder length looks dreary, and worse still: long beautiful locks hanging down like a teenager's with a mature, interesting face. The contrast is too much. Men need regular and skilled hair-cutting, plus a tidy-up of any hairs in ears or nose.

> *Gavin*, a handsome and distinguished Queen's Counsel, looks wonderful in his wig, but nature has only provided him a cuff of grey hair at the back and above his ears. Gavin resents paying a barber the full price for trimming so small a crop, with the result that he goes around with an untidy draggle of fluff instead of a neat and dignified finish to an impressive head.

Almost as bad is my brother. He spent some years in the Army, where the watchword – for hair – was 'short back and sides'. He has continued with these outmoded instructions for the last 30 years, although we tell him he looks like an ex-convict.

Most of us – of either sex – have less hair at 60 than at 17, but how much more inside our heads! Frank baldness is an unwelcome development for virile males. It is noticeable in 25% of 25-year-olds, 50% of 50-year-olds and 75% of 75-year-olds. It's nothing new: according to the Ebers papyrus, the Egyptians were trying to find a cure in 1550 BC, while Julius Caesar tried the old trick of a side parting so low that it is just above one ear.

Apart from the life-long, expensive application of minoxidil lotion (Regaine), mentioned in Chapter 2, there is nothing to be gained from lotions or potions, ultraviolet treatment or scalp massage. Various types of hair transplant are available from cosmetic surgeons, but they are not completely successful, while hair-pieces and toupees for men are rarely as convincing as wigs for women. You've only to take a look at TV personalities. Once you've sussed them out, all these gimmicks, like plastic flowers, lose any charm.

Hair-colouring, like make-up, produces the best effect if it's muted.

Françoise Giraud, the elegant Frenchwoman who was the first of her sex to become a Cabinet Minister in her country, has dark hair streaked with grey. It highlights her features. Asked if she'd never thought of covering the grey she explained that she always used a rinse diluted to blend in with the grey and complement her complexion.

We have all seen those 60-year-old ladies with hair of uncompromising blackness, which itself looks like a wig and makes the wearer resemble a witch. The too-perfect, uniform gold of dyed blonde is equally unhelpful to the woman seeking beauty: to say nothing of some crude and curious shades of red.

Grooming

Whatever special care you expend on your skin and hair, scrupulous cleanliness and grooming are musts. This applies to your clothes, too. Men in particular sometimes feel that they can relax in all directions if they retire. Don't be tempted to think that you can get by without a daily bath or shower: for one thing you are foregoing a major form of mind and muscle refreshment. Clothes equally need to be fresh. The faintest suspicion of grubbiness kills all attraction stone dead.

You are too important to allow your standards to flag, even for a single day, whether or not you think you are going to see anyone special.

Clothes catch the eye sooner than your face and hair. By now you know what suits you, so wear it – unless it is a gimmicky style that went out only a few years ago. It's OK if it's a fashion of 20 or more years past. I doubt if you are tempted, but of course avoid today's adolescent gear, however good your legs and figure. It's like the shocking incongruity of a teenage hairstyle.

Colour: it's unwise to go for the garish, but deadlier still to plump for safe, dull beige, mauve, fawn or grey, and most little floral prints. Best are the subtler shades of rust, sage, bluebell, deep rose, and for the extrovert: clear, bright red. Dark navy is kinder than black. Men can wear bolder colours, part of men's lib. Whatever else, and whichever sex, the worst way of wearing clothes is too small: this goes for shoes too. If you have expanded an inch or two, allow for it, and equally, if you've lost weight don't go around with trousers that want to slip down or have a sack appearance at the top. A particular warning to women: check how your skirts come over when you are sitting in a deep chair or getting out of a low-slung car. A flash of thigh is seldom flattering past 50.

Your figure

Your shape makes or mars the look of your clothes, and matters at least as much as your face for the over-all impression you make. It includes the way you stand and how you walk. Because of the tendency to a 'widow's hump' or the beginnings of a stoop in either sex, due to bad posture and wear-and-tear in the vertebral discs, it is essential to keep a straight back and hold your head up. Especially when you are tired or it is cold, there is an instinct to hunch up – at any age. In our case the back and shoulders won't automatically spring up straight again as they did in teenage: so we have to remind them. There is a side-benefit for the chest and lungs in an upright, confident carriage.

Any bad habits in walking tend to show by the time you reach the middle years. The persistently overweight will have developed a waddle, the woman who clings to unsuitably high heels will do the totter, while most of us slip insidiously into a slower walk, with shorter steps. Aim to swing along with decent strides if you don't want to come to resemble a tortoise. Unlike the amble, walking briskly is also a worthwhile exercise.

Of course, the main thing about your figure is its shape. You should weigh much the same now as you did on the day you got married, and you are anyway a little shorter now. The Weight Chart on page 231–2 is a guide. You should try to keep within 10% either way of your ideal weight. If you are near enough right all you need do is check the situation every couple of months, to see that your weight continues steady. Expect an upward blip at Christmas or after a holiday: taking two or three weeks to correct itself.

If you are a good deal underweight, and this is recent, have your doctor run the rule over you. If it is long-term, monitor what your weight is doing by a weekly weigh-in, and increase your intake of sweet and fatty foods: such as cake, pastry, puddings and desserts, hard cheese and meat pies.

More people are worried by 'middle-aged spread' than loss of weight, and it certainly wrecks your appearance, even your likeability, and especially if you are a man, your health. If you are seven pounds (3 kg) or more over the odds, it is time to take action: on two fronts, exercise and diet. Men usually go for the former and miss out the latter; for women it's the other way about.

EXERCISE

In general, walk instead of ride whenever it's feasible, and in any case have a brisk half-hour walk every day. Never miss the chance of climbing stairs instead of using a lift. It's a marvellous fat-burning ploy, twice as effective as jogging or swimming, time for time. Morning exercises are also a must. Start the day with 15 minutes of limbering up to keep yourself mobile, flexible and trim. Good abdominal exercises include 'cycling' on your back, lifting and lowering both legs from the horizontal and sit-ups from lying flat to touching your toes. Back strengtheners comprise lying on your front and lifting each leg in turn, and bending from side to side when you are standing.

You may like to go to a gym or class. Take advice before using the special apparatus, and avoid classes which are highly competitive or over-energetic. Yoga classes help you to be supple and are relaxing, but do not shift extra weight; aerobics can be physically too much of a strain; while weight-training benefits your muscular strength but for women tends to increase bulk and weight.

You may also like to take part in some specific sport once or twice a week. There is a selection on page 16.

DIET

Exercise tones you up, but the sad truth is that diet is the only genuine escape route from fatness. It is not bread, potatoes or pasta that do the damage but what you have with them. Fats are the culprits, and to lose weight you must cut them right down. That means omitting altogether butter and other spreads, however much reduced in saturated fats like cholesterol, and cutting out all cheese except cottage cheese or nil-fat fromage frais. Use skimmed or semi-skimmed milk, and remember that cakes, pastries and chocolate all contain too much fat for the active slimmer. The concealed fat in lamb is more than that in beef or pork; chicken has much less, especially without skin, and white fish less still.

Of course you cannot continue indefinitely holding rigidly to these restrictions, but they are necessary for a flying start. For more about diet, see pages 226–7.

Personality

Sixty-plus is the crunch period, when personality comes into its own. It is the cornerstone of charm, influence and personal happiness. It shows through your face, your eyes, your bearing, and even more in what you say and do. Unlike your physical attributes, you cannot disguise it by dress, nor have it improved by professional cosmetologists. But you can enhance your positive qualities and modify the others by taking thought.

Your individual traits and quirks, the essential 'you', are largely the result of your life experience so far, but now you can take a hand in how they develop for the future. This will make a difference to how well you adjust to your present, changing circumstances.

A good adjustment depends on reasonable self-esteem, consideration for others, friendliness, the capacity for enthusiasm and also for fortitude when it is needed. Such a personality attracts warm, even loving feelings, from other people.

A poor adjustment shows in general dissatisfaction with life, conflicts, pessimism and a tendency to regrets and resentment. This outlook is a turn-off and can set off a vicious circle of bitterness and avoidance.

WHAT KIND OF PERSON ARE YOU?

Read these questions and answer them A or B according to which part *generally* fits you best. Do it quickly: don't stop to consider. It's a first impression that's required.

1. Are you shy in company (A), or do you really enjoy being with other people (B)?
2. When you are hurt or upset, do you say so at once (A), or bottle up your feelings (B)?
3. Have you a short fuse, so that you lose your temper easily (A), or are you more inclined to react by withdrawing (B)?
4. Do you enjoy giving presents (A), or privately consider them usually a waste of money, which the other person won't appreciate anyway (B)?
5. Are you punctual and perhaps a little fussy (A), or easy-going and sometimes rather careless (B)?
6. Are you often critical about other people (A), or do you bend over backwards to give praise (B)?
7. Do you like to get your own way (A), or do you always leave it to someone else to make the decisions (B)?
8. Are you easily pleased (A), or easily bored (B)?
9. Are you interested in other people's opinions (A), or do you often find their views irritating (B)?
10. When you dislike someone do you usually show it (A), or usually manage to conceal it (B)?
11. Do you like plenty of support from other people (A), or do you enjoy feeling independent (B)?
12. Do you like to take a lot of advice before deciding

what to do (A), or do you make up your mind and do it (B)?

13. Do you think most people mean well (A), or do you believe that most of them are out for themselves (B)?
14. Do you prefer to stay in the background (A), or do you enjoy being centre-stage (B)?
15. Do you feel confident that you will be able to deal with any problems that crop up (A), or do you often feel rather helpless (B)?
16. Do you speak out when something is unfair (A), or do you usually let people get away with it for the sake of peace (B)?

ANALYSIS OF YOUR SCORE

Personality as part of your charm:
Plus points: 1B, 4A, 6B, 8A, 9A, 11A, 15A, 16A
Negatives: 1A, 3B, 4B, 6A, 7B, 8B, 10A, 12B, 13B
The other scores can count either way.

SPECIAL COMBINATIONS

1. If your score includes most of these:
   4A, 5B, 6B, 7B, 9A, 13A, 16B
   What a nice person you are, but you are inclined to mind too much about whether people like you. Risk saying what you believe, even when it is negative, and your views will be valued all the more.
2. If your score includes most of these:
   1A, 2B, 3B, 4B, 5A, 7B, 10B, 11B, 14A, 16B
   What a worthwhile person you are, but how are other people to get to know you? Meet them at least a quarter of the way, sometimes.
3. If your score includes most of these:
   1B, 2A, 3A, 7A, 10A, 13A, 14B, 15A, 16A
   What a splendidly positive person you are, but you may come over as overpowering or even bossy. Help other people to have their say.

4. If your score includes most of these:
    1A, 4A, 5A, 7B, 8A, 11A, 12A, 13A, 14A, 15A, 16A
    Of course you mean well, but you are in danger of
    being a drag. Now that you are properly adult, you
    need more practice in making your own decisions and
    taking charge of your own life. You can do it.
5. If your score includes most of these:
    1A, 3B, 4B, 5A, 6A, 8B, 9B, 10A, 11B, 12B, 13B
    What a brave independent soul you are, but you
    cannot be sure of always being self-sufficient in all
    circumstances. Why not start now to ensure against
    the risks of isolation, and work to arrange a small
    safety net of people you trust?
6. If your score includes most of these:
    1B, 2A, 3A, 4A, 6A, 7A, 8B, 9B, 10A, 12B, 14B, 15A,
    16A
    You may find that you are inadvertently upsetting too
    many people: wheel out your tact and diplomacy.

Two answers on attitude carry particular weight:
9A will open doors for you,
13B will close them.

Every person is a mix of good and bad, funny and serious,
kind and selfish. That's what makes us so fascinating, so
individual. There are bound to be some aspects which fall
short of perfect. For instance, you may find you have a
tendency to be 'careful', uncomfortably like your father's
meanness. The chances are that you learned it from him,
rather than its being built into your DNA, and inherited
inescapably. The good news is that you can modify and,
if necessary, reverse any undesirable or harmful
personality traits that have developed. It is an established
psychological manoeuvre, analogous to the treatment for
phobias.

   If someone is phobic about supermarkets, the cure is for
them to spend two solid hours in a supermarket, or else

to work up to this by small steps. By the same principle, if you realize that you are overly talkative, make a deliberate effort to encourage others to speak, instead: determine that whatever happens, you won't take over the conversation. If you are hesitant about making decisions, practise the opposite until it becomes second nature. If you are diffident, never refuse an invitation and make it your concern to ensure that other people are happy and relaxed.

There are several well-worn ways in which personality affects the style of coping with the challenging years from 60 onwards.

Constructive and co-operative response: This is the happiest and best outcome, and for this the most helpful traits are tolerance, calm, the ability to express feelings, and a readiness to enjoy whatever is available and to share it. There is a kind of adventurousness that allows you to take on new situations and new people with flexibility, broadmindedness and a generally positive approach. Aim to develop these qualities in yourself, and value them in others.

The passenger response: This type is pleasant enough, but rather passive. There is a tendency to eat, drink and take the easy way. Such a personality easily gives up, and leans on others: partner, children, friends and colleagues. If you find you may be slipping towards this attitude, because you've 'done your bit', 'earned a rest', remember that you are stopping living ahead of time. As the school reports have it: 'could do better'.

Nightmare response: None of this could apply to you or your partner, or is there the slightest possibility? The whole outlook is pessimistic, prejudiced, rigid and resentful. Such unfortunates are constantly complaining: about the young, women, men, neighbours, 'foreigners', doctors, politicians, the media, the government, the weather – you name it. They are envious of youth and compulsively, but not happily, active. No-one wants their company, yet they have good qualities, often including courage and integrity and a sense of duty. If this could be you in a few years, decide now on a different tack. It is not too late.

Upbringing and life-events have helped to shape your personality, but development, including, if you guide it, positive changes, continues indefinitely. The alterations in your circumstances likely over the next few years make it a particularly favourable period for adjusting your attitude to life, and spring-cleaning your relationships. The key is in what you do. You cannot directly change your established opinions and what you feel, but you are in command of how you act.

If, for instance, you behave as though you like your awkward relative, or really want to help single mothers, or the illiterate, other people will respond to you differently. You will be surprised to find your own feelings modifying, your interests widening.

Sybil was left comfortably off when Desmond died, but they had no children and few friends. She was a great reader, but books had lost their charm until Sybil took on the teaching of English to a Pakistani mother, who had to bring her baby with her. Her husband had mastered English through his work. Sybil had an insight on a different culture and made new contacts, and was stimulated to try new activities. She had lost her tendency to racism.

Edward had a comfortable car, a shortage of money and few contacts. He went into the mini-cab business, with a special care for the disabled: his incipient isolation was cured.

Chapter 8

Work, including retirement

'Another area of struggle concerns the laying off of over-fifty-year-olds to make way for the new generation of unemployables.'

Auberon Waugh 1992

Work and retirement. It's all down to attitudes, our own and other people's. The trouble with those who haven't lived through the experience of passing milestone 60 is that they think they know better than we do, about what we could or should do. Unfortunately their opinions are 90% patronizing and negative, with a sugar-coating of concern for our happiness. The danger is that we will be conned into accepting whatever they say.

Take work. You may love it or loathe it. You may be dreading retirement, or longing for the day when you can down tools and do what you really want with your time. You know what you value better than anyone else does, and that includes your children.

What may come as a surprise is the difference a day makes.

Take Monica: She had been widowed three years before, and was working as a ward clerk in a major hospital. The job was high on human interest, low on pay, which meant a midget pension. Monica had no intention of scraping along on next to nothing when she left the Health Service. She planned to take a better-paid post outside. On her 60th birthday the doors of her employing Health Authority closed behind her permanently. What Monica hadn't reckoned on was that most other employers would shut her out too, on the self-same day.

Brendan's crunch day was his 65th. He had been one of numerous partners in a prestigious firm of accountants, and was highly regarded. When he picked up his briefcase for the last time there was talk of private consultancy work. It didn't happen. The very people who had picked his brains so assiduously before, suddenly became 'awfully busy just now, old chap.'

You need to be prepared for a sharp change of climate to colder, in the workplace, when you touch 60. It's not just you. In times of depression and recession, especially, everyone is preoccupied with protecting his or her own job, manual to professional. Ruthlessness over retirement age – for other people – is the rule. Policies are invented and implemented to shoe-horn out not only those over 60, but, increasingly, the runners-up. A recent EEC study on the policy of a rigid, arbitrary retirement age, 'to make way for younger people' revealed that only 20% of those retired were replaced. The clue is that pensions are paid from a different fund from salaries, so it saves a firm money to off-load some senior employees and replace them, if at all, with less well qualified juniors.

Heavy physical work might reasonably be considered unsuitable past 60: but there are a vast number of exceptions, for instance in farming and horticulture.

When Jimmy retired from the Police he used his gratuity to start a small market garden. He and Jean do almost all the work, which keeps them both extremely busy, but content.

Major Burton emerged from rather discontented retirement after the great storm of 1987. Some of his services know-how came in handy and he set up as a tree surgeon.

Jean, Jimmy and the Major might be remarkable in finding satisfaction in physical work well past 60, but in the academic world extra knowledge and experience are surely accounted assets? Not a bit of it. The New Academic Appointments Scheme (NAAS for nasty) at one large London college, mentions in its forward planning statement 'the need to get rid of older employees', defined as those over 45. The car firm, Nissan, setting up in an area of high unemployment, has a policy of taking only those under 35, all grades.

This attitude might have seemed sensible in 1850, when the expectation of life in England was 41, but today it's plain daft.

Age Concern England (ACE) argues that the major criterion for being 'allowed' to hold a job should be fitness to do so. They say that ageist discrimination should be reduced by legislation:

1. To prevent the inclusion of an upper age limit in job advertisements.
2. To remove the obligatory slot for date-of-birth from application forms.
3. To abolish a fixed upper age limit for appointments to paid employment, public office or voluntary work.

Compulsory retirement in the last category seems especially ludicrous. For example, the Citizens Advice Bureau, a valuable but overstretched organization, depends on a workforce of intelligent, knowledgeable and, dare I say, mature-minded volunteers. It will not accept those past the official retirement age, yet they would appear to include precisely the type CAB needs.

Even the Police, who receive more support from our age

group than any other, have joined the witch-hunt. In 1992 they decided 'to target the middle-aged motorist' – despite the undisputed evidence that it is the under-25s who deal out death on the road.

Retirement is fine: when you are ready for it. What is damnable impudence is for employers and policy-makers to make the decision. Large, impersonal employers are the worst, operating on prejudice rather than reality. The boss who is close to his business knows (and statistics show it, too) that workers of 50 upwards are the most reliable, accurate, loyal and co-operative. They have less time off for sickness than most.

If employers, politicians and some younger colleagues need an attitude transplant, what about us? How should we react to the pressures? Ought we to accept that we've had our turn and gracefully disappear for the next quarter-century or so?

How do you see us?

1. Poor, mentally and physically disadvantaged, incompetent and whingeing: older people are a nuisance.
2. Rich and powerful, the leaders, those of experience, sound judgement and tolerance: nothing would function without older people.

Most people go for the first proposition, including our lot. Despite the facts:

We are the most important and influential group in Western culture, and even more so in the East. In the UK the over-50s will comprise the majority of the electorate within a few years. It is we who control most of the wealth of the country, including spendable income, which keeps business turning over. Our children are grown, our mortgages reduced and our needs for accommodation simplified.

Recap

60–64: The age group containing the highest proportion of high earners.

65–69: This group includes the highest proportion of leaders in industry and commerce.

50–70: Peak period for political and spiritual leadership, for example, Popes and Presidents of the USA.

The arts were never age-based, and they include the physically demanding arts of theatre and musical performance. Run your mind over Thora Hird, Nigel Hawthorne and the newly-60 Elizabeth Taylor.

All in all you are in the top group. Good to know, but there's a danger. If you feel unfairly denigrated, pressurized or patronized at work, consider your tactics before you react. The worst possible scenario is to take up a defensive stance: either a creep-type tendency with self-depreciation, or a hostile, hedgehog attitude, bordering on paranoia. Super-conscientiousness is a common defensive ploy that doesn't work. Double-checking where you didn't before, rigid adherence to every petty rule, starting work earlier and leaving later than the rest, refusal to delegate: it is all counterproductive.

You don't want to develop that irritating, elderly obsessionality which slows everything down, and drives everyone spare. If you are having a hard time, the trick is to avoid either apology or confrontation. Play it cool while you weigh up the position.

Retirement may not be what you would choose at present, but even the statesman Gorbachev couldn't withstand the combined pressures to push him out. There is no mileage in fighting a lone battle against the system. When it is inevitable, accept retirement as a necessary change. This doesn't mean giving up on yourself.

Whatever happens, you matter and it is your job to get the most and best out of your many years to come.

Retirement: from your major job so far

You will find that it isn't what you thought. It is a test, not a rest, a beginning, not an end. It is another step forwards, among a number of others you have made, each bringing new privileges and new responsibilities. Do you remember:

- Leaving your mother's side to start school. It meant managing your coat and your buttons by yourself, but it brought you a whole new world.
- Leaving school to go to college. It meant no teacher to plan every day with educational or healthful activities, but you gained the freedom of choosing what and when to learn or play.
- Graduating or completing training and starting work. It meant independence, a role, but no-one else with responsibility for your career or your leisure activities.
- And now: leaving your main job, retiring, is a challenge like you've never had before.

SUDDENLY YOU DON'T HAVE:

- A structured time-table, built round the working week.
- Somewhere to go after you've got up and had breakfast.
- Exercise of your knowledge and skills.
- The status of the job.
- Colleagues, customers and clients, people to interact with, aside from your family.
- Demands on your time.
- As much income as before.

Your major new responsibility is to organize every minute of your life, with no guidelines from anyone else; to replace some of what you have lost; and to build a worthwhile life out of your new leisure.

THE 'HONEYMOON'

As with marriage, this change of role seems strange at first, and by no means as wonderful as you'd expected. Nevertheless you have to get through it before you can begin your new life. How you deal with the honeymoon period depends on your personality-type.

A. *If you are conscience-ridden:* you will throw yourself into DIY and all the tasks you had successfully side-stepped for years.
   Maximum time: three weeks, otherwise you'll be on your knees with exhaustion.
B. *If you are conscience-free:* you will unwind, unravel, stay in bed till nine, maybe 11, wear any old clothes, slow down to a wander – and spend money.
   Maximum time: three weeks, or you'll never start the engine again.

After the honeymoon you will get back on to your life's journey. You will need a route-plan to run over the next 20–30 years: the Third Age. The Fourth Age, senior status, starts later and requires a different strategy. The first essential is an up-to-date assessment of yourself and your circumstances. Whether you aim to get another salaried job, do something worthwhile without pay, follow up a special interest, or go in for 100% holiday and leisure-living, you will need your body, mind and bank balance to work well for you.

With this in mind: check over your assets and snags, comparing yourself with how you were five years ago, and with your contemporaries. How do you rate:

1. *Bodily:* Energy, weight, joints, blood pressure etc. Do you smoke more than seven a day? Do you or could you play golf or tennis, swim, walk four miles?
2. *Thinking:* What are you interested in? Are you ever

enthusiastic? Do you fall asleep in front of the box? How well can you concentrate? Do you read anything apart from the papers or a glossy magazine? Have you sunk into a mental routine that stops all thought, or do you discuss current events and new ideas? How do you exercise your wits outside work?

Lastly: are you taking more alcohol than is good for your brain?

(*Reminder:* the recommended limit is 21 units a week for a man, 14 for a woman, and a unit is a pub single of spirits, half-a-pint of lager, a very small glass of sherry, a small glass of wine. At 60 our realistic limit is lower.)

3. *Mixing:* Outside work – what clubs, groups or sets are you part of? Have you friends you can call on for help or advice, and vice versa? What do you do to meet new people? Who might join you in a scheme for pleasure or profit?

4. *Feeling:* Are you loved and needed by some others, whether family or friends? What kind of support system do you have when things go disastrously? Who cares about you regardless? Or have you let the fungus of neglect grow over feelings?

5. *Money:* What do you own: house, capital, car etc? What unavoidable outgoings do you have? What else would you like to have or do that costs? (holidays, travel, outings, clothes, a yacht, a Goya or a greenhouse). Will your income hold up, scrape by, or plummet? Is it index-linked? Can you afford all you want, will you have to be careful or is it vital to go on earning?

Scoring system in these five areas: S for strong; W for weak; M for moderate.

In re-planning your major asset, time, consider your scores. Any W score calls for intensive care. Workaholics, for example, may have let their mixing and feeling facets fall into dreadful disrepair.

Adam had been so busy jetting across the pond in Concorde that he had become a stranger to Lesley and their grown-up children. There wasn't a slot for him in the family. He tried to buy it, but they'd grown past bribes. In the end he enrolled in the Cordon Bleu class his wife went to, and built up the relationship from there.

Muriel was the opposite. She had allowed her friends and family to exploit her warm nature, her time and energy. 'Ask Muriel – she won't mind,' was the watchword. Her own physical and psychological well-being went by the board. Trevor had already retired – and immediately immersed himself in half a dozen new projects. When Muriel hit 60 she decided to take stock: she'd become plump, dowdy and slightly breathless, and her secretarial skills had shrivelled away. It took real determination for Muriel to get her body in better shape.

A kick-start at a Health Farm helped, then the courage to take a Word-Processing course. Now she is the unpaid kingpin of a medical research team. She types up all the reports and keeps the team together – like a family.

Workaholics of either sex have especial problems with changing pace. They include the jigsaw women who have fitted in demanding home and social duties with a full-time job. Instead of feeling relief when they have 15 minutes totally free, they are bereft. Other people may feel frustrated when retirement finally arrives because of physical limitations such as arthritis or emphysema which have sneaked up. All these factors need accommodating in your New Life Plan, constructed to provide for your key wants.

Before concentrating on work or work-like things to do, some of your time and finances should be allocated to each of these three:

1. *Exercise:* Check back over Chapters 1 and 2. If you are

not keen on exercise, bear in mind that the only way of ensuring a good blood supply to your brain is by exercising your muscles. This also induces the secretion of endorphins, the brain-made chemicals that give a sense of well-being and ward off pain. So – include moderate muscle-work in your programme. Overdoing it doesn't pay.

Costing: Shooting, golf and yachting are expensive; bowls and tennis and swimming are reasonable, while walking is free – and probably the best.

2. *Brain exercise:* This is just as necessary as the bodily type: check back in Chapters 1 and 3. Springclean your current interests, revive those that have been on hold in recent years, and look for new areas to explore.

Costing: Joining special interest clubs and institutions, and taking day, evening or short residential courses can cost very little. Educational cruises or becoming a collector of, say, Victorian watercolours can cost substantially.

3. *Family, social and emotional activities:* These must have their due place, neither pushed into the background nor exploited to fill in too much of your spare capacity. See Chapters 6, 9 and 10.

Costing: Giving presents, remembering birthdays and other special occasions will be more effective if you lavish thought not money on them. Entertaining can be expensive and a trouble, but it is an important means of communicating love and friendship.

Work-related activities

Retirement isn't stopping work – as every *woman* knows. Women get practice on self-catering 'holidays' in finding that words don't always mean what they say. Retirement means a rearrangement of what you do with your time and a revision of what you count as 'work'. For instance paid or unpaid? And is the hard study required for an Open University course work? It certainly feels like it.

WHAT ARE YOU AIMING FOR?

- Paid work.
- Doing something useful and worthwhile without necessarily being paid for it.
- Developing interests, enriching your knowledge, skills and experience – as your major occupation.

Paid work

If you opt for this, don't expect it to be easy. Our age group isn't a favourite flavour. Consider your motivation.
Is it:

- *Money,* because you will definitely need it, or because it would pay for better holidays and little luxuries.
- Companionship, contacts.
- To get you out of the house.
- Search for mental stimulation.
- To avoid becoming isolated, bored.

(Apart from the first, you can achieve all these benefits from unpaid work, at the crunch.)

Points to consider:
Hours of work: what do you want and what can you realistically manage? Part-time or full-time? You may positively prefer a full-time commitment, but part-time work is often easier to find. If it is offered to you, snap it up anyway: it's a foot in the door.
Other points:

- Do you want long-term employment or only for a year or two?

- Must it be local or would you travel?
- Your chief hates about previous jobs?
- Do you need a refresher or some new training, for instance with recent technology?

WHAT CAN YOU DO?

List the main things you've done so far, both in work and outside, for instance you may have become expert at decorating, carpentry or cooking. What experience, skills and contacts have you acquired?

Other possible assets: Knowing a foreign language, car-driver/owner, willing to work flexible hours, good on the telephone or good communicator in general, fund-raising experience, for instance jumble-sales, used to mini-computers, conference and committee work, etc.

Job counselling: Either government or private firm arrangements, may give you some ideas.

NOW START LOOKING FOR YOUR JOB

Methods:
1. Your own contacts: professional institute, current or past employers, friends, acquaintances from clubs, political associations etc.
2. Advertisements.
3. Agencies.
4. Direct approach to suitable possible employers.
5. Offering your time and expertise free to learn about a business (for instance the antique trade) and to get contacts, and perhaps a foot in the door.

Curriculum Vitae: It must be neatly typed, and tailored individually to each job you apply for. Keep it short, and include only what is relevant to that job. This means being prepared to change your CV several times.

INTERVIEWS

Be ready to answer these points:

- All about your last job. Never criticize past employers or colleagues, but don't make them sound so wonderful that anything else would be a come-down.
- Did you retire early? If so, why?
- Is your health good?
- What have you been doing since leaving? Essential to have filled in unemployed time with voluntary work, not just home and holiday.
- What do you know about the organization? You need to have done advance homework for this. Secretaries are often excellent, approachable sources of information.

PAY

What do you hope to get? They are not going to pay you anything like what you have been used to: this is a fact of 60-plus life. So save *them* embarrassment. Explain that you are willing to work for a modest sum because you are keen to do this particular job, for this particular outfit. Put in the usual platitudes about difficult times for those running a business.

POSSIBLE OPENINGS TO ADD TO YOUR OWN LIST:

- Consultancy work, for instance specific projects for your former employers, for a fee, not a salary; or providing part-time expert advice to small firms that don't want a full-time tax adviser or accountant, for example.
- Temporary executive service: for bridging gaps. There is not much of this available.
- Paid work for charities. This usually develops after apprenticeship as a volunteer.

- Teaching, especially coaching: contact local schools and agencies.
- Publishing: freelance proof-reading, copy-editing, indexing.
- Journalism: if you have special knowledge, or ideas plus writing talent.
- VSO: if you are under 65, there are two-year tours of duty overseas, with living expenses.
- Temping for clerical, secretarial and some administrative posts.
- Supermarkets, chain stores, hotels and conference centres frequently have full- or part-time temporary jobs, and if you take to it you will be called upon frequently – at the last moment.
- Domestic employment as companion or housekeeper: an advantage to be able to drive.

Setting up your own business

This is exciting and can be wonderfully rewarding. It calls for an enormous commitment of time and with a couple it will absorb the energies of both. There are great financial risks, so you must get some experience in the trade for starters, and learn all you can about the complex rules of running a business. Expert guidance is essential.

Half-cautionary tale: My mother, a simple country-woman, all her learning from a village school, started her antique shop as a widow of 78. After the first year she made a small, steady income. When she retired at 90, I, with my educational and other advantages, took on the shop. I lost money so fast that I was grateful to get out at any price inside two years. I just didn't have the flair, the bargaining ability or the business sense: the parts you can't learn.

Voluntary work

This is not as easy to get as you might suppose: plenty of private and public organizations, but at least some of them seem to run a closed shop over personal participation in their activities. They keep all the fun.

Before you commit yourself to a job in the voluntary sector, CHECK:

- Whether you will be paid your expenses?
- What the job actually involves, in detail?
- What hours will you be needed?
- Who will be working with you?

Don't go for something more physically demanding than suits you, and think twice about a job that won't bring you into contact with other workers. Your aim is to replace some of the gaps left in your life by retirement, as well as giving something to the community.

ACTIVE WORK

- Meals-on-Wheels.
- Driving and escorting hospital patients, the handicapped or the elderly.
- Charity shop.
- Hospital work: in the wards, the pharmacy, the shop.
- Help with play-groups, especially in the school holidays.
- Church-based help, for instance for the homeless.
- Jumble sales, coffee mornings, sponsored projects.
- Conservation.
- Archaeology.

NON-PHYSICAL WORK

- Unpaid professional work, for instance through REACH (the Retired Executives Action Clearing

House) and its counterparts outside England.

- Counselling for CRUSE, the organization for supporting the bereaved: our age group has more experience in this field than the young.
- Help with reading on an individual basis for children of 7 to 11, or adults who've missed out.
- Befriending prisoners and ex-prisoners, the mentally ill or handicapped, or the housebound.
- Office work, telephone answering for charitable organizations: both for unfortunate people of all kinds and the arts, historical buildings, our heritage, and nature.

Back-to-school

Your choice may be to work with your brain, for the sake of knowledge rather than for a career or do-gooding. The range is limitless.

- You can join historical, literary, geographical, archaeological, scientific, musical, artistic and many other clubs and societies and take part in their activities.
- You can attend lectures, exhibitions, concerts and other types of performance.
- You can travel.

But most of all you can enrol in courses, from correspondence to day and evening classes, to residential courses, often in University settings during the vacations. Subjects may be practical like antique or china restoration or vegetarian cooking, or as creative as painting or writing poetry, or as esoteric as philosophy or ancient civilizations. All of these will cost some money, but the amounts are moderate unless you travel or collect seriously in your quest.

Financial re-planning is an essential foundation for living, for anyone over 60. We are likely to face a drop in income, and too much unplanned leisure which can be expensive. Purely pleasure pursuits – exotic holidays, major travel, theatre, opera, dining and wining and the gear to go with it can mount up appallingly. Apart from costs which can get out of hand: like a diet of oysters or ice-cream, pleasures and treats for their own sake lose their delight. They can be tiring, too.

Review all the other interests and activities that cost little or may even bring something in, and at least intersperse them with the luxury items – to derive the greatest benefit.

Some useful addresses

STUDY

Historical Association
    59A Kennington Park Road, London SE11 4JH
National Extension College
    18 Brooklands Avenue, Cambridge CB2 2HN (0223 316644)
Open College of the Arts
    Houndhill, Worsborough, Barnsley, S. Yorks (0226 730495)
Open University
    Central Enquiry Service, PO Box 625, Milton Keynes MK1 1TY
    — Leisure Series PO Box 188, Milton Keynes MK7 6DH
University of the Third Age
    BASAC, 13 Stockwell Road, London SW9 9AV (071 737 2541)

STUDY AND ACTIVITY COURSES AND HOLIDAYS

Let's Do It
   Published by English Tourist Board £3.95 (from booksellers)
National Institute of Continuing Adult Education (NIACE)
   19B De Montfort Street, Leicester LE1 7GE
   Publishes booklet of many courses (short) *Time to Learn*
Saga Holidays for over-60s (study, activity and other)
   Middleburg Square, Folkestone, Kent CT20 1AZ (0800 300 500)
Sports Council
   16 Upper Woburn Place, London WC1H 0QP (071 388 1277)

PAID WORK

Executive Standby Ltd
   310 Chester Road, Hartford, Northwich, Cheshire (0606 883 849)
Senior Service Bureau
   50 Tufton Street, London SW1 (071 222 2289)
Success After Sixty
   40/41 Old Bond Street, London W1X 3AF (071 629 0672 and 081 680 0858)

VOLUNTARY WORK

National Association of Volunteer Bureaux
   St Peter's College, College Road, Saltley, Birmingham B8 3TE (021 327 0265)
Retired Executives Action Clearing House (REACH)
   89 Southwark Street, London SE1 (071 928 0452)
Volunteer Centre
   29 Lower Kings Road, Berkhamsted, Herts HP4 2AB (0442 873311)

Voluntary Service Overseas (VSO)
   317 Putney Bridge Road, London SW15 (081 780 2266)

SPECIAL DIFFICULTIES

Holiday Care Service
   2 Old Bank Chambers, Station Road, Horley, Surrey
   RH6 9HW (0293 774535)
Arthritis Care
   6 Grosvenor Crescent, London SW1X 7ER (071 235
   0902)
Tripscope (travel)
   63 Esmond Road, London W4 1JE (081 994 9294)

GENERAL

The Pre-Retirement Association
   19 Undine Street, Tooting, London SW17 8PP (081 767
   3225)

CHECK what's available near you through your local
authority, especially for study and sport, and in your local
library and Citizens Advice Bureau for clubs, societies and
events.

Useful organizations in the USA

GENERAL

American Association of Retired Persons (AARP)
   1909 K st NW, Washington, DC 20049 (202-728-4300)
   (Free publications e.g. *Talent Bank;* 4000 chapters.
   Information on work, holidays, travel, tours, study.
National Council of Senior Citizens (NCSC)
   925 15th Street NW, Washington, DC 20005

STUDY

Arts and Aging Program
  114 Cathedral Street, Baltimore, MD 21201
Lifetime Learning Institute (LLI)
  c/o Concordia Lutheran College, 3400 1H 35 NORTH,
  Austin, TX 8705
Center for Creative Retirement
  University of North Carolina
My Turn
  Kingsborough Community College, Brooklyn
Older Adults Service and Information System (OASIS)
  St Louis and 22 other centers.

VOLUNTARY WORK

*National Voluntary Organizations for Independent Living for the
Aging*
c/o National Council on Aging, 600 Maryland Avenue SW,
  W.Wing, Suite 100, Washington, DC 20024
Retired Senior Volunteer Program (RSVP)
  806 Connecticut Avenue NW, Washington, DC 20525
VISTA (Volunteers in Service to America)
  All ages, 1 year's work with expenses.
ACTION programs (federal agency)
  Senior Companion Program, Foster Grandparent
  Program etc.

PAID WORK

Service Corps of Retired Executives (SCORE)
  sponsored by The Small Business Administration
Senior Community Service Employment Program
  run by the Department of Labour

SOCIAL AND VACATIONS

Catholic Golden Age (CGA)
   400 Lackawanna Avenue, Scranton, PA 18503 (many chapters)

Elderhostel
   75 Federal Street, 3rd Floor, Boston, MA 02112

Older Women's League (OWL)
   All over, but headquarters Washington

Retired Persons Services
   500 Montgomery Street, Alexandria, VA 22314–1563

Grandma Please
   Uptown Center, Hull House, 4520 N Beacon, Chicago, IL 60640

Useful addresses in Australia

Australian College for Seniors
   P.O. Box 1144, Woollongong, NSW 2500

U3A University of the Third Age, branches all over including U3A Brisbane, Mt Gravatt Campus, Griffith University, Nathan, Queensland 4111 (for voluntary tutoring work or study)

W.E.A. Senior Tutor Team Program – local branches
   Trains seniors to conduct their own educational programs

Learning for the Less Mobile
   Victoria

Keep Fit for the Elderly
   South Australia

Healthy Life-Style Vacationing
   Check through local Community Advisory Services* (CAB)

Australian Council on the Ageing (ACOTA)
   449 Swanston Street, Melbourne 3000, Victoria (3.663 6133) (numerous branches locally)

CAB: telephone directory will give nearest branch, but see page 211 at the end of Chapter 12.

Chapter 9

Your partner, your friends, other people

'All my coupled contemporaries are bald and discontented.'

Lord Byron, 1813

If you are married still at 60 it is proof-positive that you are made of superior quality emotional material. You must have flexibility, understanding, a sense of humour and durability. This later stage of marriage or partnership can be any of these: close, constructive, stimulating, civilized or relaxed. It may be boring, frustrating, constraining and deadly.

Don't be lulled into thinking that it doesn't take much effort, now. Even in our culture, this is not a good time to change partners, so it is important to make it work. The circumstances are unlike anything you've shared before. By now, if you've been successful parents, your children will have built up their own independent adult lives. They don't even bring home their washing. Of course you are likely still to have a healthy relationship with them: see Chapter 10 for what you should expect from them at this stage.

Your main, life-time career and that of your other half is likely to have ended, or soon will. The result is that you are thrown together, without the dilution and distraction of family, or the breaks imposed by going out to work.

You may have been looking forward to this new chance of getting to know each other all over again, to have imagined a delight in togetherness and sharing every moment. Your partner, on the other hand, may have been dreading such a change in his or her life. The wild card is that each of you will have developed and altered over time, whether it has been a 30-year marriage or a much more recent second go. Maybe your tastes and interests, your hopes and ambitions, have miraculously become identical since the starry-eyed beginning. More likely you have either grown apart by imperceptible steps, or travelled on parallel paths, each following their own affairs and occupations.

Either way, it means adjustment and compromise.

All of us cherish a dream of the future: a cottage with roses, and nature rampant; a chance to travel socially or as a twentieth-century explorer; the opportunity to follow up what you've wanted to do for years – run a pub, write music, get onto the local council, paint a house or a landscape. Your dream may centre on co-operation with your partner: his or hers may not. Often the wives of successful professional men imagine that their husbands' retirement will mean having a lot more of their company – including those social and duty occasions where the wife had to go alone and make excuses for her partner.

That's what Alice thought. Edward was Professor of Surgery at a teaching hospital, so dedicated that he was always the first to sign the consultants' arrival register – around 7 a.m. every morning. He had to retire as a surgeon, that is the rule, but Alice's hopeful plans were aborted straightaway. Edward had got himself an appointment as Professor of Anatomy in an academic department, with no hands-on operating. He was as busy and involved as ever.

Michael envisaged his retirement as a haven of togetherness, with he and Teresa tending their small garden and beautifying the house with their own hands. DIY and plant catalogues, plus TV programmes like *In Your Garden* would fill their evenings. Teresa was imagining the time when she and Michael would no longer be shackled by the demands of their jobs and they could visit faraway places and their friends in this country; they could keep up with the theatre scene, without having to get up early next morning to commute.

Moving house

An important divergence may have developed about where a couple should live. Moving is a major event, and whether to move at all is a major decision. More capital is involved than in any other facet of living. Points to mull over:

The advantages of staying where you are:
● Less stress: all moves are stressful.
● You know the area, the shops etc.
● You probably have friends, and at least you and your neighbours aren't strangers.

The disadvantages:
● It may be too big for just two of you, and expensive to heat.
● It may be lacking some features you'd like, such as a quiet neighbourhood; convenience for shops, transport, parking; a garden of the size you can continue to manage; an easy kitchen, efficient plumbing, workroom; or a luxury item, like a beautiful view.

The near-disasters arise when people choose a charming rural location, at the top of a steep hill, in high summer, then find themselves isolated in the winter. We all have friends who have upped sticks to the Costa del Sol or some other sun-haven, and then found the local medical services frighteningly inadequate when anything goes wrong.

> Eleanor's husband had bronchitis, and the warm climate on the Malaga coast would have suited him – if it hadn't been for his smoking and the drinks at the nineteenth hole. Eleanor made a social life for herself, but then she found the lump. Medical consultation in Spanish was limited to stock phrases. They'd sold their house in England, but luckily Eleanor was able to stay with her sister in London while the problem was sorted out.

'Abroad' has particular difficulties, and it is more complicated to undo your commitments there if you change your mind.

Daily routine

Another basic is your daily routine. When one or both of you were at work, this dictated such matters as getting-up time, what kind of breakfast you could have, when you ate your evening meal, the timing of your holidays and when the shopping was fitted in.

One of you may be a creature of habit, and want to continue with much the same routine after retirement. Fine if you both feel the same, but supposing the other one is more spontaneous by nature, preferring to follow the mood of the moment, especially now you've escaped the trammels of employment.

> Durley was a lawyer, precise and obsessional: up with the dawn, dinner on the dot – and none of that fancy foreign food. When he was tied to the courts' routine Madeleine

went along with it, but now she felt released. She was passionately fond of painting and if the brushwork was flowing she could not bear to stop. If Durley was hungry he could always get himself a snack: in fact most of their meals tended to be that type now. Durley was baffled and retreated to his club. Madeleine missed him and wondered what was wrong.

The key, of course, is communication. Most of us are so busy living, especially in the full flight of career, children and the mortgage that we are too tired to discuss anything deep, for about 20 years of our marriage. Communication is not chatter. It is a reciprocal expression of thoughts and feelings, hopes and fears – and finally, private dreams. If, like most couples, you haven't yet developed the habit of an open exchange of opinion and ideas, this is an excellent time to start. For example, to avoid misunderstandings and disappointment on a holiday, a weekend or an evening out, it is a prerequisite to check what the other person wants and expects from it.

Take Edgar and Mary. He was the gregarious type, she was thoughtful. When they were invited to a grand reception Edgar was happily looking forward to meeting a mix of old friends and new acquaintances: he and Mary could swap experiences when they went home. But Mary was diffident about her dress, about seeing lots of strangers: she hoped that Ed would keep with her, that they would function as a couple. Afterwards they could compare impressions of the other people.

It didn't work out. Ed disappeared into the mêlée, Mary shrank into a corner and by the time they went home Ed had drunk a little too much and Mary was sulking. Compromise is the answer, but you can't achieve that without discussion in advance. The principle applies to undertakings of any size or duration – including the blueprint for the rest of your lives from now.

It's a matter of 'give and get'. To get the talking started, say a little of what you would like to happen, but not too dogmatically or you'll kill the project stone dead. Then ask your partner how she/he envisages the holiday, or whatever, ideally. To achieve the 'free and frank' discussion that diplomats describe it is necessary to reassure your partner that whatever he says you are not going to reject it out of hand, criticize it, or blow your top. Nor can you expect the other person to be open about her feelings if you keep yours under wraps. There's no impact in merely saying what you want without giving the genuine reasons, and these are often neurotic. For example, on holiday:

> Dick didn't like lying on a beach. This wasn't because it was intellectually sterile, as he said, but because he wasn't young and handsome enough, and anyway, he was afraid of skin cancer. Jenny didn't enjoy sight-seeing because tramping around made her feet hurt, and anyway, she felt that her opinions on art and architecture would sound naive and stupid.

Because they could understand each other's very human motivations for wanting to avoid some activities, Dick and Jenny were able to plan a workable mix – before they arrived. On these subjects, and even more with matters of sex, money and relatives you will never guess correctly what another person has in mind – or heart. The only way is to make it very easy for him or her to say. For your part, it is always a mistake to suppress what you would like or what you feel 'because it might hurt' your partner. No-one thanks you for not being honest. They are more often resentful: 'Why didn't you tell me? Don't you trust me?'

Regular uncensored communication is the best insurance for a marriage, especially when it is entering the phase when each partner becomes central to the other's life. A weekly review of feelings, finance and future plans is a safety net. While the importance of communication between husbands and wives cannot be overstated, it also applies to other partnerships, and relationships with other key people.

Marital crises

They are as common as measles was when you were a child, but we haven't discovered any sure-fire immunization against them. Like tooth decay, surprisingly, trouble in marriage increases in the 60s and 70s.

PROBLEM AREAS

Competing with each other: It is natural in middle age to have a few doubts about how well you are functioning physically and mentally, much as you did as an adolescent. This time you may be wondering about any signs of wear. This can lead to an unkind competitiveness with the person whose every weakness you know, your partner. It is tempting to walk farther and faster than your other half can manage, or talk to visitors and others about subjects he or she hasn't mastered. You may take over the conversation or the activity whenever you are in public. Try to remember: always praise your partner when you are with other people and cover up if he or she says or does something that comes over as silly.

Too much togetherness: This is a potent cause of irritation. Whoever your pin-up would be, supposing pin-ups were the in-thing at 60, you would find their unadulterated company an unbearable bore. The ploy is to adulterate it. Involve other people in whatever you are doing, part of the time. We all behave with more courtesy and charm when relative strangers are watching. It doesn't have to cost any more or put you to more trouble than a 'phone call to link up with another couple or group, but it does provide a safety factor.

At the worst, if you find outsiders a pain, you will luxuriate all the more in the time with your own partner alone. Seeing other people usually helps us appreciate our own person, our own home – and even the familiar food.

Children: All the more at adult age, children can cause rifts between their parents.

> Tony found his mother a softer touch than his father, 'more understanding', he told her. When he got into a financial pickle, a frequent occurrence with his expensive ideas, his mother would subsidize him, secretly. Tony senior was furious when he found out, partly because he believed a 'boy' of 32 would learn to be more responsible if he had to sort out his own problems.

Just as when they were young, children need to see their parents with a united front. Of course it means agreeing a policy beforehand: communication.

Extra-marital affairs: Men, especially, are as aware of their sexuality after 60 as before. If someone, usually younger, shows an interest, it's a tremendous boost to confidence. At this stage, the partner at home is as familiar, and enlivening, as the wallpaper. There's no tingle if you catch his or her eye. If an evening with him means an occasional grunt from an armchair facing the TV, or the high spot of a weekend with her is a trip round the supermarket, no wonder it's refreshing to be with someone who visibly appreciates your company. In fact, it is dangerously addictive.

Don't feel guilty if you are finding pleasure and excitement outside your marriage. It's human and

natural. But do look where you are going. Such friend-
ships aren't all bad, but to break up your long-term
relationship would certainly be traumatic and might not
work for you. If you have built up remarkably good lines
of communication and understanding with your other
half, have a discussion, and in any case be frank with your
new friend, so as to sidestep any awkward expectations.
There are two ways of having a bit of both worlds: make
your new friend a friend of both of you, or else keep the
association within such bounds that your partner's way
of life and self-esteem are not disturbed.

If you are on the other side of the equation, and have
begun to realize that there is someone else in your partner's
life – STOP. Are you jumping to conclusions? Could there be
something else on his mind, for instance money? Has the
relationship been deteriorating for years, but you've only
just noticed? Even though you may feel hurt and angry,
don't make matters worse by confrontation. If you come
over as a nag, a martyr or a termagant it is extremely
unattractive and has the effect of making your partner feel
justified in finding it more fun with someone else. Unless
you want to get out of the marriage yourself, this is the
time to stay cool and collected, ride out the affair in the
high expectation that it will ultimately fizzle.

Not all affairs fade, and not all marriages are worth
preserving, apart from religious and moral tenets. If you
or your partner are considering divorce, the vital first step
is discussion with a solicitor who specializes in the
subject. You need a clear idea of what is involved, the law,
the financial aspects and your options. In divorce, nice,
reasonable individuals become grasping and vindictive.
Bearing this in mind, don't be over-generous at the
beginning or you'll end up embittered, and let your
solicitor guide you in what is reasonable for you to do or
ask. He or she is paid to protect your interests, so let him.
(See later in this chapter the section on divorce and
widowhood.)

Health

You no longer have the major responsibility for your children's health. Just as well, since it is your job, during the next couple of decades, to monitor your partner's health and happiness. This is the time to correct any unhealthy tendencies, for instance in lifestyle, and to nip in the bud any signs of physical or mental strain. You want your partner to join you in the final furlong, from 87 onwards, in as good fettle as you.

Just as your regime should comprise a balance of 'work', exercise, mental stimulus and social activity, so should your partner's. Eat sensibly together, and if one of you needs to cut down on food or alcohol, it's easier if the other one leads the way. It's a thousand times more effective than uninvited advice, however good. The physical changes to allow for in your partner are outlined in Chapter 2, and the symptoms of common disorders in Chapter 4. Bear them in mind but don't fuss.

Your partner may have a weak spot that you know about, such as high blood pressure, arthritis or diabetes. Although it is irritating and counter-productive to remind someone else about taking their pills or avoiding fatty foods, you can be careful not to increase the temptation to ignore any medical rules. If your wife has been told to cut out sugar, don't give her chocolates as a special treat; and don't encourage your husband to flout the guidelines 'on special occasions'. Invent other rewards. Particularly, don't encourage a macho man with a heart problem to over-exert himself in the garden or the house.

An area of suffering which can be misunderstood in a partner is the psychological aspect. It is easy to put someone down as grumpy, awkward, and never satisfied, when they may be sliding into a depressive illness. A loss of interest in things, not eating properly, poor sleep, minor aches and pains – may all be indications. Chronic tension, with proneness to fuss and worry about everything, or tension pains in head or stomach, is another disorder that will respond to medical treatment. The difficulty will be persuading the victim to accept such help.

Illness: Your partner may have a definite disease that impinges on your lifestyle.

> Ken has emphysema. The spirit is willing: there's so much he wants to do, but as soon as he starts off he has to stop from shortage of breath. Angie has used her cunning to get him involved in china restoration, and to train their friends to ask them out in the warm weather, but come to their house when it's cold.

> Philippa has cancer, and, as she says, the treatment is more tiring than the disease. George helps to organize their activities round the therapy periods when she is fit only to rest while her body fights the sickness. Nevertheless, Phil does have a certain amount of precious energy. Their priorities are in place so that she and George use it on what matters, for instance, in their case, seeing their grandchildren.

The writer C. S. Lewis and Joy had a wonderfully rewarding and romantic marriage, although they did not get together until she was already in a terminal phase. Most illnesses are not so dire, but a nuisance in that they impose some restrictions. You wouldn't choose to holiday in the Lake District or the Dordogne if your partner had arthritis or chest problems. The kindest approach is to skirt round your partner's impairments, without discussing them, and aim to share happily what is possible. Avoid reminders of what you might like to have done, if both of you had been able.

If you have a seriously disabled partner, review your resources: financial and friends. What you alone can give to your life partner is adult love: in most cases the sort that began with sexual attraction and carried on through parenting, home-building, and careers. You can do this most generously if you are not over-stretched by practical chores. Off-load all you can by buying in assistance and by taking up, graciously, friends' offers of help, allowing each to do a small stint. You will already have trawled through what is available through the authorities, and voluntary organizations.

A point to keep in mind is that no invalid wants to be treated as though they no longer rate as having a worthwhile opinion, on people, politics, the future. (Terminal illness is considered in Chapter 12, and bereavement in Chapter 10.)

Divorce and widowhood

These are both traumatic, but the former which need not be permanent, is often the more painful: at our age. It may be that your partner has found an attractive new option, or there has been a gradual accumulation of irritations and resentments which have become too ingrained and too complicated to untangle. Often each party takes up a rigid stance, sometimes through pride, but more often from the hurt and frustration of having tried unavailingly to put matters right.

If there seems any possibility of reconciliation, or if you would like there to be, see if you can get your partner to discuss the situation with a mediator. This person must not be a friend or relative, but someone you both accept as unbiased. Your solicitor can introduce you to one of the new breed of professionals: the marital mediators. No outsider can impose solutions on you, but he may put things in a different perspective.

Sometimes the illness or death of the elderly parent of one partner can put a marriage off balance because of divided loyalties.

Before his marriage Jack had been very close to his
mother, who had been widowed when he was 11. She had
been an independent, dynamic woman whose strength he
had admired and relied upon, and she certainly hadn't
leaned on him or interfered when he married. At 85 she
had a stroke: not fatal, but it limited her physically and
dented her self-confidence. Jack felt he owed it to her to
do all he could, dropping in on his way home most
evenings, doing odd jobs for her at weekends. Bunty had
never got on with her mother-in-law. She resented what
she saw as Jack's desertion, and her mother-in-law
compounded the situation by having a series of mini-
strokes which kept Jack constantly anxious.

There were several possibilities. Bunty could have made
caring for the old lady a joint project, or together she and
Jack might have come to the conclusion that his mother
would be safer with round-the-clock professional care, in
a 'home' or hospital. Jack might have tried harder to
mobilize, through the GP, the Social Services and Age
Concern, as much help as possible and ration his own
input so that Bunty could be sure of some of his company.
If a couple can communicate they have a good chance
of recognizing potential pitfalls, and getting some degree
of control of them. This stage in a marriage is a
particularly propitious time to find a deeper, more
satisfying meaning in life – together. Earlier you had some
separate and other joint objectives: you will have
achieved these or they are no longer relevant. You can
have down-to-earth new aims, for improving your home,
providing practical support for a good cause, seeing
Niagara or relatives you have neglected. Then there are the
more spiritual goals, often ideas you meant to follow up
years ago.

Maurice had a Jewish grandmother. He had always played
down that side of his heredity, but when he had more time

to think, the rat race behind him, he began to remember the stories and sayings the old lady had told him as a child. He and Marion, his wife, became fascinated with the culture they had ignored, and its wisdom.

The Colbys had lost their only son in a senseless accident, at the age of 20. They'd thrown themselves into work and charities and got through the years somehow; but only now, in their 60s, were they able to talk honestly about their guilt, and their resentment towards each other for surviving. At last they were able to achieve some peace of spirit and feel a part of the great human family: all the parents and all the children.

This may be the time when you and your partner can share the excitement of exploring new territory, not only in human values but in art, music, science and nature.

If you are not so fortunate, but find yourself bereaved through death or divorce, you have a difficult period ahead, but one that you can expect to come through stronger and wiser than before. The worst pangs of widowhood diminish in six months, but the tormenting mix of emotions following a divorce can straggle on for three years. For one thing, your friends and relatives will be divided, and not altogether sympathetic. However blameless you were, you'll feel that you've done something wrong. Your social standing, especially if you are a woman, has plummeted, and your children, whatever they say, won't really see things your way.

There will be a brief period of sympathy for you, if you are widowed, and if you are a man you may be overwhelmed with hot meals and help: at first. Long before you have recovered, other people will have shifted their attention to something new. It doesn't make much difference now, which type of disaster you had: you don't fit in as you did before. It is not all bad, however.

Gradually an appreciation of your glorious freedom

grows in you. Life provides new experiences, and there is no-one to stop you looking into new opportunities, or dumping activities you don't enjoy.

If you have gone through a divorce because you had found someone different and special, and wanted to spend your life with them, this also can have problems. Obviously your earlier marriage had continued for longer than the present relationship, so you will have to unlearn a lot of how you ran a joint life before. There will be a new set of values and ideas to adapt to, so it is doubly important to make communication in depth a top priority. Enjoy a fresh chance of enduring happiness and harmony with someone you love by starting it right this time.

Whether you are divorced or widowed and on your own, talk about it freely to start with, but pipe down for certain after three months maximum – or you'll not only lose your friends, you'll drive yourself into a neurosis. Use the commonsense and courage that come with maturity, and set to work to create a worthwhile life.

Friends

At 60, even more than before, friends are your richest resource. Take care of them and be super-tolerant of their foibles. Your current age is like adolescence: a time of change and uncertainty about the future. You need your peer group for support: they are the only people who really understand – just like when you were 17.

Friends who live nearby are particularly precious, so let them know they are appreciated. Friends of retirement age are notoriously unreliable, not in character, but in what they do. They may decide to take a holiday for six months in Australia, go on safari to Africa, or defect permanently to settle in a villa on some Mediterranean costa. Some of them take up hypochondriasis like a profession, and some unluckier ones may become ill. Either way, you need a reserve force for replacements. This means going out of your way to meet new people locally, and from acquaintances try to build new friends.

Socialize, go to meetings of any sort, entertain at least a little, and be ready to join in for the sake of the company, sometimes. There is no time yet in sight when you can sit back and let the world come to you.

Chapter 10

Children, grandchildren and other relatives

'The children despise their parents until the age of forty, when they suddenly become just like them, thus preserving the system.'

Quentin Crewe

Politician Margaret Thatcher went on about the family, saying it was a 'good thing'. Margaret Mead, the anthropologist didn't know whether it was good or not, but that it was inescapable. However society tries to organize life, for instance by kibbutz or commune, a sense of family always seeps through. We might as well accept it: and make it as pleasant as possible for ourselves.

Ours is the age of tolerance and tact, the essentials for construction work: building bridges and mending fences. If there is a coolness or a schism or a lack of contact for no special reason, this is a time to review the situation, and make some tentative moves.

Sybil's mother-in-law had always been unpleasant: no girl would have been good enough for her Ben. In the early years of the marriage she had pointedly invited her son over without Sybil, criticized the way she brought up the twins, and said she had no thought for money. In fact, Sybil earned a reasonable salary. The maddening part was that Ben seemed blind to his mother's blatant unfairness.

It wasn't surprising that Sybil had avoided having anything to do with her, as soon as the children were old enough to visit her on their own. But now she was 83, and Ben said she had a dicey heart.

Wally had side-lined his sister, Anna, rather similarly. She had always been a bossy-boots and a know-all – although she was only three years older than him. The final straw was when their father died. He had made Anna sole executor of his will, and left the lion's share of the money to her. It was so unfair, when Wally had a wife and three children, and Anna had only herself to look after. They'd hardly spoken since the day of the funeral.

Sybil and Wally could have let matters slide, but there were dangers in that course – for them. Suppose Sybil's mother-in-law were to die, or Anna's arty-crafty ceramics shop to go down the chute and leave her stranded? They'd feel guilty and it would be too late to put it right. They both used the excuse of Christmas, Easter or a birthday would have done equally well, to make the first overtune. They'd determined not to expect a miracle. In the event, Sybil's mother-in-law responded surprisingly graciously. Anna is still on her high horse, but Wally feels better anyway. As his wife remarked they had the real riches of children, and Anna must have envied them, too.

Most of the time, of course, we are concerned with getting on harmoniously with the relatives with whom we do have contact. We are in a wonderful position: old enough to understand what the younger generations are experiencing because we've been there, and young enough to supply strength and support to the generation ahead of ours. There is one golden rule for dealing with relatives of whichever age group and whatever degree of closeness. Show your affection for them plainly.

Even if 'they must know you love them', or if you've proved it by helping them in practical ways over the years, it is still, and always will be, necessary to say the words. You love them and value them. If you've always been the undemonstrative type, particularly when your children grew up, this is a time to reconsider. Don't miss out on hugging your youngest and oldest relatives, and try if it is acceptable for the middle range. If ever you need to comfort someone, that's what they need. If you have a married son, be sure to greet his wife first, and most warmly. Sons-in-law, because of tradition, can be dodgy. Let them set the pace.

Family relationships become more important now: for both men and women, but rather differently.

Men and their children

Men, during their 60s and 70s, are likely to be in the transition phase: from being absorbed in a full-time, major, working role to having a relaxation of demands on their time. Even if you struggle against it, change is inevitable: like the end of a play or a concert. This is the moment when men decide to refresh the kinship ties which they may have neglected for the last quarter century. Hardworking fathers are often motivated by their family's needs, sacrificing their leisure to be able to buy their children a better education, better holidays – all the privileges they'd wanted for themselves.

The pay-off for parents can be startling: grown-up children with beliefs, interests and attitudes different from ours, with lifestyles to match. The final straw is that *we* jar on *them*, no matter if we got on wonderfully well with them when they were really children. It can be hurtful, but it is not due to lack of affection, just a clear demarcation of the generation gap. A particularly tricky situation is that of a father and son in the same business. They are bound to have divergent ideas, and each may be convinced that the other's judgement cannot be trusted.

The younger man 'hasn't had the experience'; the older one 'hasn't moved with the times'. A father staying on past retirement age because he enjoys the work, as well as feeling he's the best person to be in charge, is a recipe for resentment and friction. Like two women in a kitchen, two men directing one business or professional practice have to show enormous restraint over offering advice, let alone active interference, especially from older to younger.

These are the negative aspects, but there's plenty that is good and heart-warming. There can be periods of easy companionship and understanding between father and son, and for most daughters their father was their first love and holds forever a precious place in their mind.

Women and their children

Personal relationships and the family are naturally more important to women, the experts in matters of emotion. The disadvantage is that any conflicts are more upsetting. At 60-plus it's up to us to be the peacemakers in the family, yet often we are the focus of everyone's discontent.

There is always a degree of rivalry between mothers and daughters or daughters-in-law. If you are aware of the danger you are half-way to avoiding it. Remember that, as a mother, anything you say that sounds even faintly disapproving will be taken to heart. Our children's generation is not nearly as secure as they seem, and our task is to boost their self-confidence. This involves considering the effect of any personal remark before you make it. Will it give the younger person a lift?

If it hasn't come about naturally already, now is the time to work for co-operative and harmonious relation-ships with your married children's in-laws. It is one of the most beneficial things you can do for your children and grandchildren in these days of easily-breakable marriage. Your child's in-laws may be totally at odds with you – in religion, culture, politics, financial status and the more subtle values.

> Jonathan was the Greens' only son. They weren't orthodox, but nevertheless they had always assumed that he would marry 'a nice Jewish girl'. It was a sadness when he chose Laura, the daughter of divorced parents with no religious beliefs and no sense of family. Her mother had remarried to an American and came over once a year 'to keep up with the grandchildren'. Jonathan's parents had been formally polite, but distant. Laura's mother always outdid them in gifts.

This was a snag when seven-year-old Kim was found to have a spinal tumour. Jonathan and Laura were devastated. They needed solid support, not two sets of parents competing. Rivalry between grandparents, particularly grandmothers, is harmful to the very people they want to help.

It is natural for a mother of our age to enjoy seeing her own child without always having the partner as well. Unfortunately seeing one without the other invariably leads to tension in their relationship. Make a rule to treat your married child and partner as a unit. Daughters-in-law will be resentful if you see your son on his own; sons-in-law will blame your influence for any disagreements with your daughter.

It's human nature to find pleasure in your children's company although it can be irritating at times. But it is equally normal for them to enjoy their independence from you, and to value their privacy – from you.

What children want from their parents

At this stage, what they most want is that we should be happy, involved in interests of our own, self-sufficient, and expecting no commitment from them – but instantly on tap with a sympathetic ear or solid help. This is normal, not unnaturally selfish.

If you feel like complaining about something with every justification, your children will see you as a 'moaner'. Being pathetic doesn't arouse the tender care you may long for. At heart, of course, they care about you, but they don't want an uncomfortable pressure on their conscience. You will be less of a worry to them if you have friends of your own age, and things to do which keep you busy and which you enjoy. This is crucial if you are widowed or for some other reason flying solo. Lose the word lonely from your vocabulary: it's a turn-off.

> Maisie fell into the mistake of depending on her son Michael for company and conversation: it didn't seem worth bothering with anyone else. She was shocked when he told her that he was going out to Saudi for a three-year stint. His wife was going with him, naturally.

One of our ongoing responsibilities to our children is to provide them with a model of how to cope with older adulthood. How else can they learn? An incidental which more often applies to men after retirement is appearance. Good grooming and attention to clothes – including fashion – is a way of boosting your personal confidence and respect from others. It's fatal to dig out something 'you've hardly worn' from a bygone style: like flared trousers or waisted jackets. Even if you are not expecting to see anyone except the family, never think that you don't matter. That time never comes.

Grandchildren

There is a delicious warmth and affinity between grandchildren and grandparents. Youngsters can confide in them comfortably, especially in the difficult years from puberty through adolescence. Grandfathers are always welcome and in the increasingly frequent situation of a mother bringing up her children alone they may fulfil a vital role. Both boys and girls, but especially the latter, need a male presence to develop a rounded understanding of society. Even if your own son or daughter has a wonderfully rich family life with their partner, a grandfather is always regarded as a special asset.

Not so grandmothers. It's that female propensity for each, at any age, to want to be the best wife, the best mother, the person most loved and needed by the children and men in the family. Grandmothers are walking through a minefield. The first mine is the temptation to give advice. It will be seen as interfering, critical and out-of-date if you spontaneously suggest anything to do with childcare. No question that you know more than a tyro mother, but keep it to yourself. If you are actually asked for advice, offer it well-sugared with praise for how admirably your daughter or daughter-in-law has managed.

Another trap is if your son chances to discuss with you some problem with a grandchild. No matter what you say, your wise words, as relayed by your son will stand a 99% chance of upsetting his wife.

Another pitfall for grandmothers is becoming too popular with your grandchild. Children are devastatingly frank with their opinions, having no hesitation in declaring that their grandmother is nicer, makes better food, and is altogether more fun than their mother. Don't slip into being an indulgent grandmother, and frequently remind the youngster how good and kind and clever and pretty his mother is.

'You never used to let *me* stay up late,' said Emma bitterly, when her mother pleaded for grandson Tim, aged six, to be allowed to watch a James Bond film.

The fourth mine involves both grandparents. It concerns generosity. One of the most satisfying experiences in life, especially in a marriage, is for a couple to work hard and by their efforts to be able to provide advantages or treats for their child. It siphons off this joy and sense of achievement if a well-meaning older relative just writes a cheque, instead.

'I didn't even want him to go there,' complained Adam, when young Stephen's fees for a prestigious public school were guaranteed by his father-in-law. Sarah thought Adam was being selfish and petty, putting his pride ahead of their son's interests. They couldn't have a proper discussion about where to send the boy, because it had been taken out of their hands. Adam was ungrateful and ungracious. Sarah told him so.

It is fine to be generous to your grandchildren, so long as you make certain to preserve the dignity of their parents. It may not be as enjoyable for you to give them the money to buy something for the children, rather than turning up laden with magnificent gifts, but it really gives more pleasure. And if you are paying for, for instance an educational journey or the plain school fees, do it in a businesslike way, and never speak about it again. On the other side of the coin, don't allow yourselves to be pressurized into providing funds which you may need for yourselves later on.

Your overriding duty is to make sure that your own future is secure. You are not likely to make a fresh fortune over the next few years and you may need a contingency fund.

Older generation relatives

If your parents, or at least your mother, or an elderly aunt or uncle are looking to you, they will be definitely old. This means that you are the strong, clever, competent one now, whose judgement is sound and whose know-how is up-to-the-minute. Most major decisions are likely to be better made by you: even in the teeth of opposition from the older person. A common source of conflict arises when a relative becomes too frail or too muddled to fend for herself, yet insists that she wants to stay in her large house. The danger, especially if you are a daughter, is that you will be manipulated into taking on too big a practical commitment, ostensibly in the short term.

Nothing is more destructive to harmony at home than an older relative requiring constant care, and either moving in and destroying all privacy, or causing non-stop anxiety if she is on her own.

Loving, and seeing the old person as often as you yourself feel like it, can do nothing but good. Tying yourself down and exhausting yourself with regular chores is lunacy. If you are always available, the doctor will slide all the responsibility over to you, rather than go through the time-consuming and frustrating process of arranging professional help. Likewise the Social Services.

> Irene's mother was 90 and blind, a splendid character. She insisted on living alone with her cat, listening to Radio 4 full blast. She did not admit to deafness. She didn't want any Home Help, Meals-on-Wheels, or Social Worker shoving her nose in, thank you. She could manage perfectly well with a bit of help from her family. Her family was Irene.

Irene was on a treadmill, shopping and cooking for her mother, including the cat's fresh haddock. She went round every morning to help her mother dress, and clean round the fishy-smelling flat. She gave her mother breakfast on this trip, leaving her lunch on a tray. In the evening, as soon as she and Sidney were home from work, they would set off with the old lady's supper, and Irene would get her into her nightclothes. Weekends were for washing and ironing and shopping. Sidney, either a saint or a wimp, accepted the situation. It was Irene who developed an ulcer with the strain. There was no let-up for her, the ulcer got worse and she was finally admitted to hospital as an emergency. The three weeks in hospital turned out a blessing. Her mother didn't have to leave her flat, but enough help was arranged by the doctor and the local authority to enable her to cope without Irene. She came to enjoy the various new personalities in her life; and Irene became a valued occasional visitor.

The moral is never to start something no one human being can sustain.

ALZHEIMER'S DISEASE

While AIDS is the plague that haunts the younger generations, Alzheimer's is the plague that gets to the older generation. Only a minority are affected, but if you have older relatives it is sensible to know something about this disorder. It involves a progressive loss of brain power, first affecting the recent memory. Mercifully the sufferer is unaware and unworried.

'I have an excellent memory – always did have,' said my Aunt Rose, in her 90s. She had a complete blank for the visit of a favourite granddaughter half-an-hour before. We noticed that she had burned several of her saucepans, because she forgot she'd left them on. Worse still, she might turn on the gas and forget to light it. Time had got jumbled, and one night after midnight, she set out with her shopping trolley, another worrying event. Clearly she was at risk on her own.

If you have a relative like Aunt Rose, there are far-reaching decisions to be made – and someone else has to make them for her. Irene's mother, no younger than Rose and blind, could manage with helpers who came in part-time. An Alzheimer victim, like my aunt, requires care and supervision for 24 hours, seven days a week. The relatives have to consider whether they could provide that level of attention, if it were otherwise feasible to have the old person living with them. Experience shows that is almost impossible – and always stressful.

Live-in minders, if there is room in the patient's home, are expensive, difficult to keep and at least two are required to cover each other, plus extra arrangements for holidays. That leaves residential care. The ordinary 'homes for the elderly' will only take Alzheimer's at the beginning of the illness, but it is likely to go on for some years, with increasing disablement. There is a range of private nursing homes which provide full cover: some are excellent, others appalling. All of them cost a lot. The best arrangement, if and when the doctor can arrange it, is a place in a State-run or recognized facility. Most of them are good, but, as with the private places, it is essential to check them out – for kindness of staff, expertise, clean kitchens, and well-cared-for residents.

Since a person whose brain is failing cannot fend for themselves, or tell you about problems, you need to monitor their progress. Smooth the way for the old person you love by being appreciative of the staff, for her, and if you have criticisms, couch them in terms that cannot give offence. Encourage your relative to take the same attitude, as far as she is able, then the staff will spend time with her.

The same principles apply if you have a frail elderly relative who is mentally fit but has to have residential care for physical reasons. One of my older friends, an ex-headmaster, looked round the pleasant and welcoming establishment he was to live in. 'I loathe this place and everyone in it,' was his instant verdict. Fortunately the nurses understood, and within three weeks he had settled happily: the average time it takes, I was told.

However aged or physically incapacitated someone may be, you will help them to retain a feeling of worth by asking their opinion and by showing an interest in their past experiences. It's a matter of allocating some time, slowing the pace to suit the older person, and remembering that he or she may not have as many opportunities for conversation as you. This kind of thoughtfulness, plus affection, is the greatest gift for our parent generation.

BEREAVEMENT

With relatives of the older generation, this experience is likely. It isn't an illness, but there are definite symptoms and a typical course. The death of a parent, even if they've led a full life, or had been suffering a distressing illness, is always upsetting. There's an illogical feeling of guilt. How do parents always manage to do this to us? And anxiety. This is a chilling reminder that we are now in the front rank for dying. Mixed up with the other emotions you can expect a tinge of relief, but often no feelings at all come through at first. There's just shock and disbelief, a kind of numbness.

Gradually this gives way to uneasiness, about nothing in particular, and waves of sadness, and tears. This is normal and healthy: a necessary part of grieving. It's a help in the long term to give way now and express your feelings – in the company of other people. It is healing to talk endlessly about the dead person, every detail, over and over. If it is your friend who is bereaved, don't try to keep off the subject or distract them. Expressing loss and often anger that the person has died should not continue longer than two or three months, or it develops into a habit.

Jean still says: 'I blame the doctors.' Her mother died six years ago – aged 98. The bonus from this loss is that the shake-up provides a new chance to reconstruct your life and your values, and a chance to practise mutual supportiveness with relatives and friends. If you really have no-one, obtain support through your doctor and voluntary agencies like Cruse.

Chapter 11

You are of value

'Regret is dead, but love is more
Than in the summers that are flown,
For I myself with these have grown
To something greater than before.'

Alfred Lord Tennyson 1850

There is no doubt about it: we are valued. Not by everyone, but an increasing number of important sections of society. The half-affectionate terms that are bandied about: Oldie, Wrinklie and Woopie (well-off older person) don't have the denigratory overtones of Yuppie, Dinkie and yobbo applied to the juniors.

Politicians value us for our votes: there are a lot of us. You'll have noticed how promises about pensions, special benefits and improved health care for our age group fly around near election times. Party headquarters, especially locally, are manned – or womanned – by those over 60, with a little help from the youngsters.

Holiday and travel firms woo us for our custom, especially since we are not tied to the school holidays, and are more likely to be able to travel midweek. There's never been such a plethora of packages geared for our lot: you are even allowed to take a 50-year-old with you, like taking a child to an adult category film. The holidays range from coach trips at the cheap end to Mediterranean or round-the-world cruises in the top range, or interest holidays in Greece or Italy or the further reaches of our own country. A major gripe is the supplementary charge for singles, which so many of us are, in this modern world.

Educators have also got us in their sights as potential students. They dangle before us day or evening courses, and brief residential blocks, often using University accommodation. That's the key: they gain the delights of teaching students who want to learn, and whose life-experience enriches the classes, and also the cost-efficiency of using the facilities when the undergraduate population are on vacation.

Professionals of the fashion industry want our bodies – to clothe. Their traditional market, the teenage-plus is shrinking: ours isn't. Thigh-high, psychedelic, skin-clinging designs are doomed unless we come to want them. This is unlikely, but there's a crying need for an imaginative approach to what would suit us. What's on offer in under- and over- and foot-wear for us is inadequate in choice and often dull. Too many styles hark back to the dark ages or are hideously unflattering if you're over 30. Both sexes need to be more demanding in this area, despite our normal tolerance.

Magazines ostensibly directed towards the under-40s have always had a much more mature readership. We are so versatile we can relate to any age group. There are a handful of journals aimed at the recently-retired, all rather dreary, but the launch in 1992 of *The Oldie* shows a welcome trend: up-beat and witty, and meant for us.

Property developers certainly court us, with hopes of a share of our life-savings. Retirement homes, designed for convenience, mainly small, are mushrooming in clusters: some with central social and restaurant facilities. There are others in apartments, with or without service. In the State sector there is so-called sheltered housing: usually tiny flatlets with a warden to keep an eye on everyone's welfare. You are probably too young and too healthy to qualify. These special developments can be useful if you are communally-minded rather than individualistic, prefer the company of your own generation and older, or have a tiresome physical problem. Otherwise it is generally happier and healthier to be part of the real, mixed, rough-and-tumble world of all ages. That's not to say that you shouldn't make use of all the labour-saving devices available.

Another group who may seem especially keen to help us are the financial experts: they want us as clients and investors. Unfortunately any proposition that sounds too good to be true probably isn't. The plausible and apparently prestigious expert may not be an intentional villain, but an unrealistic optimist.

Charitable organizations also want our money, but also our unpaid time and expertise. This part can be a boost to the conscience and also provide a social spin-off.

All these people value us mainly for what they hope we can give them: unlike Prince Charles. He sees the Third Age, between the child-rearing and work-oriented Second Age and the Fourth Age of dignity, contemplation and a lessening of responsibilities, as a precious reservoir of practical and theoretical knowledge, wisdom and benevolence and the potential for further development. We are of value to the community and for ourselves, he believes. We have a choice of opportunities with which to construct lives that combine leisure and rewarding activity: a chance to realize our best selves.

Consider these late-flowering plants, who did much of their best after 60: writers such as Goldsmith, Iris Murdoch, William Douglas Home; philosophers Bentham and Dr Johnson; composers Handel and Tippett; poets Betjeman and Milton; politicians Mandela and Churchill; artists Leonardo and Rembrandt – and actors, lawyers and churchmen galore. Just a sample.

As Lord Chelmsford remarked to the House of Lords:

'It's never too late to begin, and it would appear that it's never too late to end.'

A sad situation is that in spite of our having so much to offer that is needed, too many people literally retire. They withdraw from involvement, stagnate – and wilt. For example, it is quite surprising that only 10% of those retiring do any kind of voluntary work, but the 10% provide a most vital service. When volunteers of all ages are caught up in a project with a joint purpose, the ugly barriers between the generations dissolve. Agencies to help the homeless, or foreign students, political parties especially at election time, charities to preserve our heritage – all provide just this scenario. The older group tend to manage the financial and clerical work, the telephone and cutting the sandwiches while the younger ones do the racing around. Fund-raising is for everyone. In these circumstances it is obvious that when the young look at the old and the old look at the young, they are looking at themselves.

Recent surveys show that people begin to be afraid of growing older from about age 16. The 16-to-24-year-olds see old age as being well under way by 60. From 25 to 50-plus they plump for 60 as the start, but somewhere in the 50s the goalposts begin to move forwards. We know that 60 is just another birthday and nothing frightful happened to make us suddenly decrepit. People of 75 are adamant that old age starts at some time well ahead of them.

Top fear about getting older is poor health: but this is the era of medical miracles. New hips, new knees and re-conditioned big toe joints are standard; 70% of cancers are curable and some avoidable, and chest diseases are on the wane. Heart disease is already well down in the USA, and the UK is sure to follow: but at worst there are pacemakers and by-pass operations, revolutionary treatments. The previously unpopular specialties of geriatrics and psychogeriatrics are now in the vanguard.

Lack of funds is the next most important anxiety that people have about getting older: especially those in the 30-to-40 decade. It doesn't seem such a worry, surprisingly, from 50 upwards. For those over 75, fewer than 5% rate it as significant. They have learned that while 'loadsa-money' can buy some special treats, there are plenty of others available. When he was staying with the Queen at Balmoral, Gladstone, who was then in his 80s, indulged his great pleasure in long walks. Victoria did not approve, but she found her enjoyment in involvement with people, and correspondence with her children.

We are lucky to have such a nice long ride on life's roundabout. Prince Charles, in his early 40s, has already lived longer than his great great great grandfather, Prince Albert. It gives Charles, and us, so much more time to do and see and learn and feel things. At this point, unlike the fledglings starting out on adult life, we are no longer strangers in an unfamiliar world. We know our way around. In 60-odd years we've experienced most of what life can throw at us: disappointments and losses, rewards and surprises, delight and despair. Whatever crops up now, we'll know how to cope.

Having come this far, we can expect to enjoy a period as long as from cradle to college or first job. Whatever base of knowledge and skills you have already, there is all this extra time to add to it, without the bind of trying to build a career or the responsibility of dependents. However few or many friends you have, there's time to develop new ones. If you are shy, remember there's no need to make an immediate impression: you are not starting school.

Demographically we have a particular problem. Our age group is being added to faster than any other, but it is skewed. There are so many more women than men. Just as employers need to get their act together over recruiting staff for the nineties and 2000 onwards, using the age groups available, so society requires a re-jig of attitudes and conventions. We who are over 60 now must be the trendsetters. Those who have husbands have a responsibility to help those on their own to join in where it is still awkward for a woman to go alone. We should keep an eye open at airports and the like for ladies of our age who have all the complexities to deal with alone.

Those who are widowed or otherwise on their own must guard against finding it 'too much bother', often a euphemism for too frightening, to attempt anything more adventurous than turning on the TV. Why shouldn't a woman go to a restaurant, a theatre, a wine bar or a concert on her own? People with services to offer must learn to make us feel welcome – on our own. Of course you can pair up with a friend, which makes such sorties easier, and usually more fun. One cruise firm, at least, runs holidays in which mature male partners are provided – for the dancing and as dinner companions. The snag? You can't take them home at the end.

Welfare: the very word conjures up dreary vistas of benefits, concessions, grants and sheltered housing. The State provides some help, but never enough, and never warmly personal. Family feeling and neighbourliness flourish better away from the big cities, but to transplant yourself to a country village now may help in the long run, but for a year or two you may be even more isolated. The best bet for most of us is to develop links where we live already. It's a question of being alert to local opportunities that you may have been too busy to notice before.

We have considered your value to various organizations, and your value to yourself for all the pleasure and interest and usefulness in you. But you are worth most of all to other people. You know and understand, from your own experience, what it's like to be a child, or an adolescent. You can relate to other people's problems of love and work, or being a parent. You can remember what it feels like when things go wrong – and when they come right. You have all this first-hand knowledge, yet you are young enough to be lively and flexible in outlook – with a facility for compromise.

You, and we like you, are the most worthwhile people around: QED.

Chapter 12

The last chapter

'Death closes all: but something ere the end,
Some work of noble note, may yet be done . . .'
Alfred Lord Tennyson

The last chapter of a life, like that of a book is as momentous as the first. It draws everything together, completes the story and reunites us with nature, and all those who've gone ahead.

Ben Travers, the playwright, died at 94. In a broadcast the year before he suggested his epitaph should be: 'Here is where the fun begins'. Most of us don't view death quite as enthusiastically as he did, since partings are always tinged with sadness. However, Dame Cicely Saunders, who has probably known more dying people than anyone, writes reassuringly: 'Death is almost always preceded by a perfect willingness to die.' My personal experience with patients, friends and relatives, has been comforting. Most people slip away so easily that you can hardly believe it has happened, while those who have fought courageously against an illness, often for the sake of others, seem as though they have found relief and tranquillity when they finally relinquish the battle.

If it is your partner or someone else close who is reaching the last phase of life, you have two vital tasks. One is to help make this a warm and worthwhile experience for you both. The other, even more important since the first depends on it, is to keep care of yourself. You are going through a straining, testing time, and will have further responsibilities in the future. Your emotional and physical welfare must have top priority. Get all the support you can from relatives, friends and professionals. Do mind your diet: nourishing, easy-to-digest, regular and unhurried meals. You must make the time for sleep, fresh air, exercise and some distractions. All this because your ability to cope is crucial.

What only you can provide for your partner is your love: others can supply physical care. Nurses, hospital, hospice and nursing home staff all run on a shift system: so no-one gets exhausted. Don't try to compete.

It may be helpful to you as well as your partner if you can understand the emotional impact when a person begins to recognize that this time he – or she – is not going to recover. People react in different ways but the likely sequence starts with a hollow pretence that the situation is not as serious as it is. This gives the invalid time to adjust internally. Next he may feel anger. It is anger at the illness, but unfortunately this is usually expressed towards other people, often doctors and nurses, but most hurtfully it may be you. Although it sounds like it, it doesn't really mean blame and dislike for a person. The anger is sometimes followed by a 'bargaining' phase: the ill person, whether he is religious or not, may pray that he will live long enough to see a grandchild, visit the Grand Canyon, or see one more springtime. Think twice before embarking on a trip out of range of familiar medical help.

To all, inevitably, comes sadness: at the prospect of leaving and losing the dearest and most valued in life. At this stage it helps to talk about feelings, fears, regrets and relationships – and to smooth any wrinkles. Finally comes acceptance of death: this you should not deny, but share in, all the way.

The whole fundamental experience will drain you, but also make it easier for you, when finally you follow.

Practical arrangements: when someone dies

Of course it's a shock when it happens, however much the death was expected. You'll feel anxious, but there will be people to help you, and every one of them will try to be considerate and supportive to you.

WHEN SOMEONE DIES AT HOME

First of all, telephone the doctor. Don't delay, even if you are certain the person is really dead. If the doctor has seen his patient very recently, and the death was peaceful and expected, he may decide not to visit immediately, but delay, for instance until the morning, if the event occurred in the night. If you think cremation is a likely choice, mention this straightaway. In that case the doctor has to arrange for a colleague to see the dead person, too.

As soon as you have informed the doctor, make yourself some tea, and if there is no-one else in the house, get hold of a friend, neighbour or relative to keep you company, at least for a few hours.

The doctor will give you, or any other relative on the scene, the *medical certificate of death*. This states what he believes was the cause of death, when he last saw his patient alive, and whether he has seen the body. There is no charge for this certificate, which is not the *Death Certificate* proper, which is provided by the *Registrar of Births and Deaths*. The doctor will also give you a *Notice to Informant*, which lists the people eligible to register the death with the Registrar. This has to be done within five days. The doctor, or his receptionist, will give you the address of the Registrar for the address where the death took place. He or she will also supply, if you need it, the name of an undertaker.

The doctor may also offer you – literally – three or four sleeping tablets, to ensure that you get some rest the first night or two after such a major happening in your life.

Telephoning the undertaker is your next task. As an expert in such situations, he will be reassuring, informative and practical. Will you want the body to be laid out at home or would you prefer it to be at the undertaker's chapel of rest? In hospital, it may be done by the nurses, otherwise it is the responsibility of the undertaker's staff. It consists of making the dead person tidy and comfortable, and is best done as soon as possible.

You will need to have a discussion about the funeral or cremation, including, from the start, the cost involved. The undertaker has to wait, before moving the body for a special green certificate which you will get from the Registrar: the *disposal certificate.*

Registering the death: This must be done with the Registrar whose area includes the place the person died, which is not necessarily his or her home address. When you, or another person on the Notice to Informant list, go to the Registrar, you must take this Notice with you and also the medical certificate. If you can, take the dead person's birth certificate, marriage certificate and National Health Card also. The questions the Registrar will ask include:

- The date and place of death, and the home address if this is different.
- The sex and full name of the dead person, including her maiden name, for a woman.
- What had the person's work been, and was he or she retired?

The Registrar copies the cause of death from the medical certificate, and also records the doctor's name and qualifications. He will also want to know the dead person's marital status (single, married, divorced or widowed), but this does not figure on the final certificate. The Registrar will check with you that he has written down everything correctly in his draft. If you agree, he will then make an entry in the Register, in special long-life ink, give you a pen to sign it with, and he will sign it, too.

Death Certificates: These are copies of the entry in the Register. You are likely to need more than one, for probate, insurance and other official purposes. They cost £2 per copy currently, during the first month after the death, but the price goes up later.

WHEN SOMEONE DIES IN HOSPITAL (OR NURSING HOME)

The nursing staff will probably have informed you of the death, or confirmed it if you were already there. If someone else was named as next-of-kin, they will be informed. In most hospitals a special clerk looks after the arrangements with the relatives. If the death occurred out of office hours an appointment is made for the following day, when the procedures will be explained to you. At the same time, the patient's belongings will be given to you: you may like to take a case with you, to use instead of a plastic bag. The hospital doctor will have supplied the medical certificate of death, and the clerk will give a list of local undertakers: you have to arrange with the undertakers to take the body away from the hospital.

Registering the death is the same as when someone has died at home, except that it must be done at the office of the Registrar whose district includes the hospital.

If the death was unexpected, or associated with an operation the hospital must inform the Coroner: usually this is just a formality. The Coroner informs the Registrar, and then the death is registered in the ordinary way.

Organ donation

The only useful parts from an older donor are the corneas: the transparent front of the eyes. It doesn't matter whether the dead person had good sight or not. The doctor at the hospital must be informed at once, for the corneas need to be removed within hours of the death. This can be done in the home, if that is where the death occurred.

Final resting place

The usual choice is between burial and cremation. The green disposal certificate from the Registrar must be given to the undertaker, now funeral director, before he can proceed.

Burial: For Jewish people a Burial Society commonly takes over after the death is registered. Otherwise, regardless of religion, or lack of it, everyone in Britain has a right to a burial place in a churchyard if there's room, but more often in a cemetery. The funeral director, of course, knows the ropes, and there are various fees associated with burial, in whichever place, and also for the Church Service.

Cemeteries: The majority are non-denominational and run by the Local Authority. Costs and facilities vary.

Cremation: Various forms have to be filled in: one by the next-of-kin, three by doctors. Funeral directors and crematoria have the forms. Crematoria don't operate at weekends. The fees include the use of a non-denominational chapel, with a choice of chaplain. It is not obligatory to have a religious service, but unless you say so, it will be assumed that you want it. The ashes can be collected a day or two later, and the undertaker usually does this, and provides an urn, unless you prefer the crematorium to scatter the ashes in their Garden of Remembrance.

You can keep the urn, have the ashes scattered somewhere specific, or buried in a churchyard or cemetery.

Memorials, tablets etc can be considered at leisure.

Announcements of the death are usually made in a national and a local newspaper. The undertaker will do this for you, if you prefer. Information about the funeral, where to send flowers – or 'No flowers', is included in this notice.

After the funeral: It is a kindness to provide light refreshments for the mourners. Funerals are emotionally exhausting, and it brings things back into perspective to share some ordinary food and chat with others.

Business matters

You cannot legally do anything with the dead person's property until probate has been granted, if there is a will; or you have letters of administration, if not. You must inform the bank, post office and building society if the person had accounts with them: the money will be frozen temporarily. The Tax Inspector will also want to know of the death; Pension and Allowance books should be returned – but do keep a note of the numbers. For any problems or worries about your home, consult the Citizens Advice Bureau or a solicitor.

Support

Your friends, your relatives and your family doctor are all likely to rally round – at first. You may also benefit from help through Cruse Bereavement Care or the National Association of Widows.

Ends and beginnings are as natural and inevitable as the waves of the sea. The experience of parting from someone you love is universal. All people, prosperous or 'having to be careful', famous or just ordinary, suffer and survive such losses. It is something we share with our great human family. Be proud to be a member of it and kin to the good, like Florence Nightingale, the beautiful, like Cleopatra, the courageous like Neil Armstrong and Stephen Hawking, and the lovable, whom you know.

These may be useful:
What to Do When Someone Dies. Which Consumer Guide, Hodder and Stoughton (London) 1991, £9.95.

Cruse Bereavement Care, Cruse House, 126 Sheen Road, Richmond, Surrey TW9 1UR.

The National Association of Widows, 54–7 Allison Street, Digbeth, Birmingham B5 5TH.

USA

Registering a death is somewhat simpler than in the UK, but requires the same information. The doctor signs a certificate which the funeral director fills out, with your help. He then sends it to the appropriate district (township, borough, city) and it is filed where the person died, not in the place where he lived if that is different. There are minor variations between states.

These may be useful:
Widowed Persons Service of the AARP (American Association

of Retired Persons) 1909 K St NW, Washington, DC 20049 (202-728-4300)

Living/Dying Project, PO Box 357, Fairfax, CA 94730

St Francis Center, 5417 Sherier Place NW, Washington, DC 20016

Rainbows for All God's Children (local chapters), 1111 Tower Road, Schaumberg, Il 60173

Local papers advertise counselling, support and self-help groups for the bereaved

Area churches often provide or sponsor bereavement counselling and support groups.

AUSTRALIA

The procedures in Australia are based on the British system, with a central Registry of Births, Marriages and Deaths. There are minor variations in the different States but the doctor or hospital staff will give you the information and addresses you need locally. Information on legal requirements, and such matters as benefits can be obtained through these departments:

N.S.W.: Department of Youth and Community Services
Victoria: Department of Community Welfare Services
Queensland: Department of Welfare Services
W.A. & S.A.: Department of Community Welfare
Tasmania: Department for Community Welfare
N.T.: Department of Community Development
A.C.T.: Welfare Branch, Department of Territories and
   Local Government
Community Advisory Services (CAB): all over, including
Canberra: CAB, Suite 6, 17 Trenerry Court, Western 2611
Brisbane: CAB, 168 Ann Street, Brisbane, Queensland
Perth: CAB Western Australia, 78 Murray Street, Western
   Australia 6000

Association for Civilian Widows of Australia
   239 Gregory Terrace, Springhill, Queensland 4000
   (07.831 5810)

Marriage Guidance Council
   159 St Paul's Terrace, Brisbane 4000 (07.839 9144)

Appendix

All about eating

'The true essentials of a feast are only fun and feed.'
Oliver Wendell Holmes

Eating is not only refreshment for the body tissues but a restorative to the spirits. You can expect to repeat the delightful experience three or four times a day, indefinitely. Eating with someone else means sharing life with them, for at least as long as the meal lasts, or maybe throughout a marriage.

Two changes may arise after the big Six-O. If you are on your own you may feel it's hardly worthwhile to bother for one, and the quality and variety of what you eat falls off. On the other hand, finding yourself with more time and sufficient money, you may slip into the way of spending more of both on the easy pleasures of food and drink. There is a tendency anyway in our western culture to consume more fat, sugar, meat, alcohol and tobacco, and to reduce the intake of cereals, potatoes – and physical activity.

So it is the second of the two unhealthy eating styles of 60-plus that is the likelier hazard. Professor Roy Walford, an American gerontologist, advocates what he calls his 120-Year Diet. It is basically an essay in the rewards of restraint. The Hunzas, who live in the Himalayas, are the most outstanding of the long-lived races, reckoning a century as just another birthday. Retirement, if at all, comes later. These people run on about half the calorie count here, comprising a little meat, chillis, peppers and apricots, washed down with wine and water.

Professor Walford recommends for the westerner 2000 kilocalories a day for adult men, reducing to 1900 at 60, 1800 at 80, with 200 kcals per day less for women. These amounts nourish without throwing a strain on any system, and specifically save the immune system from wear, and delay the development of arthritis, cancer, heart disease, cataract and dry skin.

Walford's allowances presuppose a moderately active life and these vital statistics:

	Height	Weight
MEN	178 cm (5'10")	70 kg (154 lbs/11 st)
WOMEN	163 cm (5'4")	55 kg (120 lbs/8½ st)

Obviously, if you are just as active now as you were 30 years ago, or your height is very different from the norm, you should adjust what you eat. Aim to stick within 1.5 kg, 3½ lbs either side of the ideal.

US guidelines

The United States Departments of Agriculture and of Health have produced seven dietary guidelines, for general use:

1. Eat a variety of foods.
2. Maintain an ideal body weight.
3. Avoid too much saturated fat and cholesterol.
4. Eat foods with adequate starch and fibre.
5. Avoid too much sugar.
6. Avoid too much salt.
7. If you drink alcohol, do so in moderation.

By far the commonest nutritional disorder found in the over-60s is obesity, but where there are deficiencies they are likely to be in vitamin C, folates or iron. At this stage you need to cut down on fats and sugar, but not to omit milk, eggs, meat, fruit and vegetables. Before we get on to specific diet suggestions, let's consider . . .

All you need to know about vitamins and some minerals

Vitamins and certain minerals are vital to health and a protection against particular diseases, including some cancers. All the diets suggested comprise a balance of nutrients, including these special factors. Only minute quantities are required, because they are so powerful. By the same token, an excess can poison you: mothers have often overdosed their precious babies out of love and ignorance.

You are not likely to harm yourself in this way if you take your vitamins and minerals the natural way – in foods, not potent pills. You require exactly the same amount now as in all your adult life: there is no virtue in having extra. Vitamins come in two groups, those dissolved in water and those contained in fats or oils.

WATER-SOLUBLE VITAMINS

Vitamin C (ascorbic acid): You need this to make collagen, the elastic supporting tissue in your skin, blood vessels and also scar tissue. It has another important role in stress, both physical and emotional, via the adrenal glands. It probably has a generally beneficial effect on the working of the brain and the immune system, and it has recently been shown to be a preventive of stomach cancer.

It seldom causes toxic effects, but in susceptible people it can increase the likelihood of bladder stones, or the accumulation of iron in the body.

Recommended intake: 60mg a day.

Where to find it: Fresh fruit, especially blackcurrants, guavas and citrus fruits; salads, especially green peppers, watercress, lettuce and tomatoes; and rapidly boiled vegetables, especially sprouts, cabbage, cauliflower, broccoli and spinach. Canned and frozen vegetables do not lose much of the vitamin.

The B group
Thiamin: This is necessary to make proper use of carbohydrate foods, our main source of energy. A shortage of thiamin can occur in heavy drinkers, who cannot absorb it properly. The effects are loss of appetite, easy fatigue, irritability and a feeling of anxiety.

Recommended intake: Depends on the amount of carbohydrate.

Where to find it: Wholewheat, pulses, nuts, pork. Rice and white flour use up more thiamin than they provide, while raw fish destroys it.

Niacin (nicotinic acid): It is useful for the health of the skin, breathing and digestive apparatus.

Where to find it: As well as eating it ready-made in food, we can synthesize this vitamin from the raw materials. Major suppliers are liver, kidneys, Marmite, beef extract, eggs – and instant coffee.
  Nicotinic acid tablets make the skin flush and are sometimes given to pep up the circulation in chilblains.

Riboflavin: This substance enables the body cells to make efficient use of the oxygen provided by breathing.

As with thiamin, the amount needed depends on how much food there is to be processed.

Where to find it: The usual natural sources are liver, cheese and eggs, but the highest concentrations are found in meat and yeast extracts.

Vitamin B12 and related substances. These are vital for the manufacture of the red blood corpuscles. A shortage leads to pernicious anaemia, Bernard Shaw's disease, and also a form of paralysis and psychosis. He was kept fit by injections of liver extract, despite his denunciation of meat-eating!

Recommended intake: 3 micrograms a day, but if you've run short you need it by injection.

Where to find it: B12 is unique in that it is not found in any plant: vegetarians get their supplies from milk, eggs and cheese. Other sources are meat and poultry, and especially liver. Strict vegans probably get a minute amount from micro-organisms and moulds contaminating their food, but they run a high risk of serious illness.

A parasite in raw fish, enjoyed by the Japanese, can infect humans and use up their supply of B12, and some drugs prevent its absorption – for instance, colchicine for gout, and slow-release potassium.

Folic acid: A lack of this causes a form of anaemia, with weakness, tiredness and poor concentration. Older people, those living on their own and Asians living on rice are susceptible. It is not absorbed properly if you are taking some of the anti-epileptic medicines, HRT or too much alcohol.

Where to find it: Liver, broccoli, savoy cabbage, runner beans and oranges. Cooking tends to destroy it.

Vitamin B6 (pyridoxine): This exhibits all-round metabolic usefulness.

Recommended requirement is 2 mg daily.

Where to find it: cereals, meats, green vegetables and fruits.
No adults run short of this vitamin, unless they are taking a particular anti-tuberculosis drug or possibly oestrogens (in HRT). The biggest danger is that TAKING TOO MUCH can cause incapacitating illness.

FAT-SOLUBLE VITAMINS

Vitamin A (retinol): This one keeps your skin healthy and, more important, the retina of your eye, especially for night vision.

Where to find it: Milk, butter or margarine, cheese, egg yolk, liver. Its precursor, beta-carotene, from which it is made in the body, is found in carrots, green vegetables, sweet potatoes and apricots: so eating these is just as good. It is destroyed by sunlight, for instance in dried apricots, but protected by Vitamin E – in wheatgerm and sunflower seed oil, especially.
It is very rare for anyone to run short of retinol, but excess – from halibut or cod liver oils, or too much liver, can cause headache, hair loss, itchy skin and loss of appetite.

Vitamin D: The sunshine vitamin. It is manufactured from the oils of the skin by the action of ultraviolet light. A dark skin is a disadvantage for this – a reason for the fair colouring of the Scandinavians. Not many foods provide Vitamin D.

Where to find it: Fish liver oils, of course, and herrings (including kippers) and containing a lot less – sardines, margarine and eggs.
If, for any reason, you are deprived of all sunlight for a long period, your doctor may advise the synthetic vitamin, about 10 micrograms a day, plus milk and

cheese to supply calcium. Too much Vitamin D is dangerous, especially to the arteries, but it is necessary for strong bones. It enables the body to absorb and use calcium. Osteoporosis, a loss of substance from the bones, is common in older women who take too little exercise. It can be complicated by osteomalacia, a kind of adult rickets, with loss of calcium, if there is a shortage of Vitamin D. An X-ray is the certain way to check.

Vitamin K: The blood cannot clot properly without this, which could make the smallest injury troublesome.

Where to find it: Fresh, green, leafy vegetables especially. There is no likelihood of running short of it except in cases of serious disease, or prolonged use of antibiotics, with a poor diet.

Vitamin E: The precise value of Vitamin E is still a mystery, and it has been used, without any real evidence for its efficacy, for menopausal symptoms, muscle aches and skin problems. We know for sure, however, that together with Vitamin C it is protective against stomach cancer.

Where to find it: Wheatgerm, sunflower seed, palm and various other vegetable oils of the polyunsaturated variety. A major source is margarine, but no-one runs short of Vitamin E on a normal diet.

MINERALS

There are only two minerals of concern to our age group: calcium and iron.

Calcium: The amount of calcium the body requires is the same throughout adult life. It is needed for tough bones, and also for the functioning of nerves and muscles. Vitamin D is necessary to be able to make use of calcium in the diet. The two main reasons for running low in calcium are dietary and hormonal.

Post-menopausal women, 55s and over, lose a lot of calcium in their water, probably because of their reduced production of the sex hormone, oestrogen. It may be helpful for some people to take HRT from 55 onwards. Steroid medicines are another hormonal cause of a reduction in calcium.

Where to find it: Cheese, especially hard varieties, milk, sardines, and in the UK anything made with white flour, which contains added calcium.

A snag in 'healthy' diets with plenty of wholewheat, oatmeal and fibre is that they contain phytic acid: which prevents the absorption of calcium. This is one important way in which white bread beats brown, even 'dephytinized' wholemeal. Some Asian diets are particularly low in calcium.

There is no evidence that extra calcium as medicine has any effect on the bones in osteoporosis: regular exercise and HRT are the best treatments we know.

Iron: This mineral has a key role in enabling haemoglobin, the red pigment in blood, to carry oxygen to all the body tissues. It is an essential component of all-over well-being. The commonest form of anaemia is that resulting from a shortage of iron, and it is estimated that between 5% and 20% of those over 60 are anaemic. The causes are:

1. *Reduced intake*, especially in those on their own: it is easy to slip into simplifying the diet, by missing out on meat and vegetables and relying on bread, spreads and sweet foods.
2. *Loss of blood* from slight, pesistent bleeding, from: piles; taking aspirin regularly; hiatus hernia; diverticulosis; peptic ulcer.

Where to find it: Liver, meat, eggs, (not fish), All-bran, treacle, dried fruit, plain chocolate.

Green vegetables, despite their reputation, are not a worthwhile source of iron, but the vitamin C in fresh fruit aids the absorption of iron from other foods. Alcohol helps similarly. Tea reduces the absorption, and although wholewheat contains plenty of iron it is poorly absorbed.

Iron tablets are a cheap, effective treatment for anaemia, but may cause side-effects: nausea, heartburn, and either constipation or looseness.

Zinc: This is fashionable, but of no practical importance unless you are a chronic alcoholic or a bran-freak: someone who takes ridiculously large amounts of the stuff. Zinc deficiency leads to skin problems.

Where to find it: Oysters, meat, wholemeal.

SPECIMEN DIETS

Useful measures for constructing a diet:
1   oz   =   30 g
3½ oz   = 100 g
4   oz   = 120 g
Slice of small sliced loaf ⅔ oz = 20 g
Half-slice of large, thick-cut loaf ⅔ oz = 20 g
Cup = 8 fl oz = 237 ml
Tablespoon = ½ fl oz = 18 ml

Normal diet for man 1900 kcals; for woman 1700 kcals (at 60+).

Rates of usage:	kcals/hour
Sleeping	65
Sitting	100
Standing	105
Slow walk	200
Carpentry	240
Swimming	500

Running 570
Fast walk 650
Walking upstairs ....1100!

In all cases, take three meals a day with drinks between. All the nutrients you need are provided by the diets.

Normal diet

BREAKFASTS

Essential not to miss; all with coffee or tea and semi-skimmed milk; fruit juice as well, optional.

1. Porridge or oat bran porridge and honey and semi-skimmed milk. Fruit.
2. Muesli and semi-skimmed milk.
   1 slice toast with margarine and marmalade.
3. Grilled tomatoes or mushrooms, or baked beans on wholemeal toast and margarine.
4. Cereal and semi-skimmed milk, with banana, handful of sultanas or prunes.
   1 slice toast and margarine.
5. Fromage frais, fresh fruit and crispbread.
6. Boiled or poached egg, or slice of grilled bacon, with 2 slices of toast and margarine.
7. Scrambled egg and tomatoes on toast with margarine.
8. 1 yogurt, 1 fruit and 1 slice of toast, spread and preserve.
9. 3 fresh fruits, crispbread, milky drink.

   For a man add to each an extra slice of toast, spread and preserve.

Note: a standard portion of cereal is about 3 heaped tablespoonfuls, and of porridge 4 level tablespoonfuls.

ELEVENSES

Coffee, tea or juice, with 1 semi-sweet biscuit if wanted.

LUNCHES

All with juice and/or coffee or tea to follow.

1. Cheese including tofu, fish, meat or egg: 2-3 oz, in a wholemeal bread sandwich or with a roll and very little margarine, with salad or vegetables.
Fruit or a light dessert.
2. Jacket potato with meat, fish, cheese, egg; coleslaw.
Yogurt or fresh fruit.
3. Baked beans on toast and spread.
Fruit.
4. Vegetable, beef and tomato or other soup; roll.
Yogurt and fruit.
5. Ham roll and tomato.
Ice-cream and biscuit.
6. Chicken, egg or cheese with pickle and tomatoes, and 4 rye crispbreads.
Fruit.

TEA

Drink.

SUPPERS OR DINNERS

Starters: Optional: any of these:
Crudités; fruit juice; orange, melon or grapefruit without sugar; garlic mushrooms.

Main courses: Mineral water or glass of wine (see below). Basically 4 oz of meat, fish, cheese, egg, poultry, with vegetables or salad, for example:

1. Stir-fried chicken and vegetables.
2. Tandoori chicken.
3. Fish curry with rice.
4. Steak and onions, jacket potato.
5. Braised liver and onions or leeks.
6. Grilled white fish and vegetables.
7. Vegetable curry and brown rice.
8. Baked ham and vegetables.

Vegetables include potatoes, but not fried or roast, or a roll may be taken instead, with a little margarine.

Second course:

1. Baked apple, with sultanas and ice-cream.
2. Stewed fruit and ice-cream or yogurt.
3. Fruit sorbet.
4. Fresh fruits.
5. Cheese (2 oz) with crispbread or fruit.

Coffee with semi-skimmed milk.

Alcohol

Not more than 2 alcoholic drinks a day – if possible. A drink is a small sherry, a pub measure of spirits, a small glass of wine, half-a-pint of lager or beer. Spritzers are a taste worth acquiring for health. These drinks are taken for their social effects, not that they have any nutritional value.

Hangovers: These are caused by lack of water in the system, and by the congeners (other constituents than alcohol) in the drinks. In order, the worst hangovers come from brandy, port, rum and red wine, and rather less from white wine and gin, with vodka having the least effect of all.

Diet to build up your weight and strength

On waking: Tea with sugar and milk, biscuits.

Breakfast: Juice, cereal with milk and sugar, egg or bacon or kipper, roll or toast with spread and preserve.

Elevenses: Milky drink, with biscuits, bun or doughnut.

Lunch: 3 oz meat, fish or cheese including vegetarian, or 2 eggs in sandwich or roll, salad or vegetables. Dessert or pudding: for instance open flan, sponge, upside-down cake.

Tea: Tea, sandwich, cake.

Supper or dinner: Juice or soup; 4 oz meat, fish, chicken with potatoes, other vegetables or salad. Dessert or pudding; cheese, spread and biscuits. Fruit if wanted.

Bedtime: Milky drink and biscuits or sandwich.

Bland diet

After a digestive upset, or during an illness. This must be a matter of trial and error, but in general you should avoid:

1. Alcohol, tea, coffee, cola, meat extract drinks.
2. Pickles, curries, spices.
3. Fried foods.
4. Twice-cooked foods.
5. Sausages, bacon, pork.
6. Fatty fish like sardines, mackerel, herrings.
7. New bread, wholemeal bread.
8. Rich puddings.
9. Excess of sugar and sweets.
10. Raw vegetables.
11. Dried fruit, nuts, unpeeled fruits and tomatoes.

Reducing diet

Useful in overewight and late-onset diabetes.

GENERAL GUIDELINES

3 meals daily with drinks between, including bedtime.

- No butter, margarine, cream, whole milk or fried food.
- No *made-up* meat dishes, like pâté, burger, sausage, meat pie.
- No *made-up* egg dishes, like quiche.
- No chocolate, avocado, milk pudding, pastry.
- No biscuits except crispbreads.
- Be moderate with fruit juices, even unsweetened, and any alcohol.

YOU MUST HAVE

Two of these daily: Fish, chicken, egg, meat, cottage cheese, fromage frais, soya dish, yogurt, Edam, baked beans.

Carbohydrate 3 times daily: Bread, toast, roll, crispbread, potato, rice, banana, porridge, bran cereal.

You may take freely: Fruit, salad, vegetables – with low-calorie dressing or non-sweet pickle.

SPECIMEN MEALS

Interchangeable, e.g. breakfast for lunch or supper.

Breakfasts: Drinks with semi-skimmed milk, with each.
1. Three fresh fruits, e.g. apple, orange and banana.
2. Porridge made with half-a-cup of oats, water or fruit juice to moisten.
3. 1 yogurt, 1 fruit, 1 crispbread with touch of honey.
4. Stewed, unsweetened prunes and bran cereal.

5. Baked beans on slice of toast. Tomato or apple.

Lunches: with juice, or coffee with semi-skimmed milk.
1. 2 slices bread, or a roll, spread with low-cal salad dressing, piled with salad and chicken or prawns.
2. Cottage cheese, salad, salad dressing, roll.
3. 4 rye crispbreads, low-cal soft cheese including vegetarian, salad.
4. Ham and baked beans, half-slice of toast. Plum, nectarine or 4 grapes.
5. 4 rye crispbreads, chicken or ham, pickle. 1 fruit.

Supper or Dinner: 2 courses with mineral water, and coffee afterwards.

1st course:
1. Chicken, cottage cheese, meat, ham: with jacket or boiled potato and salad or vegetables.
2. Soup full of vegetables, roll or toast, reduced-fat or tofu cheese.
3. White fish or prawns with rice or boiled potatoes; watercress or similar.
4. Casserole of meat and root vegetables, stock cube (no fat); bread.

Salads are lettuce, endive, Chinese leaves, peppers, tomatoes, onions, grated carrots, cucumber.
Vegetables – any.

2nd course
1. Yogurt.
2. Ice-cream (not cream ice).
3. Sorbet.
4. Fromage frais.
5. Soya dessert.
    All with or without unsweetened raspberries, strawberries, sliced banana, or stewed fruit.
6. Fresh fruit and 1 sponge cake (as used in trifle).

Bedtime: Drink made with semi-skimmed milk.

High fibre diet

For constipation or diverticulosis.

On waking: 2 cups hot tea.

Breakfast: Half-a-grapefruit, or juice.
Porridge, bran cereal or muesli. Stewed prunes.
Wholemeal toast or oatcake, with margarine and chunky marmalade.

Elevenses: Coffee or tea, piece of fruit.

Lunch: Vegetable soup, wholemeal sandwich with salad, or celery, cheese and roll.
Fruit. Drink: mineral water, juice, tea, coffee.

Tea-time: Tea, oatcakes, crispbread.

Supper or Dinner: Meat etc. with jacket potato, salad and vegetables.
Fresh fruit or fruit pudding with dried or other fruits, or rhubarb.
Do not neglect to drink plenty with or after the meal.

Bedtime: Wholemeal biscuit and drink.

If bloating occurs avoid lentils, baked beans, natural bran, and legumes.
In general for the high-fibre diet avoid white bread, pasta, rice, cake and pastry.

Low cholesterol diet

AVOID: Liver, kidneys, brain, fish roes including caviare, shrimps, crisps, most nuts, gravy, canned soups, cheese, coffee whiteners, eggs, meat pies, sausages, fat meat, luncheon meats, chocolate, ice-cream.

The following foods are acceptable (unless you are overweight, in which case care is needed with the sweet ones): bread, porridge, cereals, pasta, potatoes, rice, lean meat, preferably chicken or veal, all vegetables, salads and fruit, polyunsaturated oils and margarines, skimmed milk, walnuts and pecans, jam, jelly, marmalade, marshmallow, honey, all types of fish.

Breakfast: Juice, grapefruit, stewed fruit.
Cereal or porridge with skimmed milk.
Toast or roll with margarine and marmalade.
Coffee or tea with skimmed milk.

Elevenses: Drink as above, plain biscuit.

Lunch: Chicken (no skin) or lean meat or cottage cheese salad with roll and margarine, or similar sandwich. Fruit. Drink.

Tea: Tea and skimmed milk, fruit or plain biscuit.

Supper or dinner: Poultry, fish or lean meat, with pasta, rice, boiled or jacket potatoes or roll, and vegetables.
Fruit, or dessert made with egg whites, skimmed milk and polyunsaturated fats.
Coffee and skimmed milk.
Juice, mineral water or a *small* glass of wine with the meal.

This diet is good for those with many heart or artery problems. You should also aim at keeping your weight a little below average. Whatever the reason for a high level of cholesterol in the blood, this diet is useful.

Low sodium diet

May be advised for those with high blood pressure and some heart problems.

AVOID table salt, salt in cooking water for vegetables, ham, bacon, sausages, corned beef, smoked fish, cheese, ketchup, sauces, salt butter, white bread, rice crispies.

USE spices and herbs for flavouring, also sugar, jam, fruits, marmalade.

Hurry through anything else, but eat in an oasis of tranquillity. It needn't take long. Whatever and whenever we eat, each meal or snacklet is relief for mental or physical strain, and when it is shared, an affirmation of friendship or love: the natural way to celebrate or to console.

Acceptable Weights for Women

HEIGHT			WEIGHT (average)	
metres	inches		kilograms	pounds
1.45	57	(4′9″)	46	102 (7st 4lb)
1.48	58	(4′10″)	46.5	103 (7st 5lb)
1.50	59	(4′11″)	47	104 (7st 6lb)
1.52	60	(5′)	48.5	107 (7st 9lb)
1.54	60½	(5′½″)	49.5	110 (7st 12lb)
1.56	61	(5′1″)	50.4	112 (8st)
1.58	62	(5′2″)	51.3	114 (8st 2lb)
1.60	63	(5′3″)	52.6	117 (8st 5lb)
1.62	63½	(5′3½″)	54	120 (8st 8lb)
1.64	64½	(5′4½″)	55.4	123 (8st 11lb)
1.66	65	(5′5″)	56.8	126 (9st)
1.68	66	(5′6″)	58.1	129 (9st 3lb)
1.70	67	(5′7″)	60	133 (9st 7lb)
1.72	67½	(5′7½″)	61.3	136 (9st 10lb)
1.74	68½	(5′8½″)	62.6	139 (9st 13lb)
1.76	69	(5′9″)	64	142 (10st 2lb)
1.78	70	(5′10″)	65.3	145 (10st 5lb)

Acceptable range: from 4kg (8½lbs) below average to 7kg (15lbs) above average.

Figures based on British and American standards.

Acceptable Weights for Men

HEIGHT		WEIGHT (average)	
metres	inches	kilograms	pounds
1.58	62 (5′2″)	55.8	124 (8st 12lb)
1.60	63 (5′3″)	57.6	128 (9st 2lb)
1.62	63½ (5′3½″)	58.6	130 (9st 4lb)
1.64	64½ (5′4½″)	59.6	132 (9st 6lb)
1.66	65 (5′5″)	60.6	135 (9st 9lb)
1.68	66 (5′6″)	61.7	137 (9st 11lb)
1.70	67 (5′7″)	63.5	141 (10st 1lb)
1.72	67½ (5′7½″)	65	144 (10st 4lb)
1.74	68½ (5′8½″)	66.5	148 (10st 8lb)
1.76	69 (5′9″)	68	151 (10st 11lb)
1.78	70 (5′10″)	69.4	154 (11st)
1.80	71 (5′11″)	71	158 (11st 4lb)
1.82	71½ (5′11½″)	72.6	161 (11st 7lb)
1.84	72 (6′)	74.2	165 (11st 11lb)
1.86	73 (6′1″)	75.8	168 (12st)
1.88	74 (6′2″)	77.6	172 (12st 4lb)
1.90	75 (6′3″)	79.3	176 (12st 8lb)
1.92	75½ (6′4½″)	81	180 (12st 12lb)

Acceptable range: from 5kg (11lbs) below average to 8kg (17lbs) above average.

Figures based on British and American standards.

Recommended reading

Exercise Beats Arthritis, Ian Fraser (Thorsons, 1992)

Better Sight Without Glasses, Harry Benjamin (Thorsons, 1992)

Coming Off Tranquillizers and Sleeping Pills, Shirley Trickett (Thorsons, 1991)

It's Up to You – Overcoming erection problems, Warwick Williams (Thorsons, 1989)

Prostate Problems, Jeremy Hamand (Thorsons, 1991)

Osteoporosis, Kathleen Mayes (Thorsons, 1991)

HRT, Patsy Westcott (Thorsons, 1993)

Food Combining for Health, Doris Grant and Jean Joice (Thorsons, 1984)

Overcoming Depression, Caroline Shreeve (Thorsons, 1987)

Index